11/12/2014

S0-AEZ-124

2008

The Trading Method That Can Make You Rich

....

Roy Kelly

Published by:

TREND PRO INC.
2533 N. Carson Street Suite T326
Carson City, NV 89706
www.trendpro.com

ISBN 0-9760715-0-9

Library of Congress Catalog Card Number 2004111375
PRINTED IN THE UNITED STATES OF AMERICA

Second Edition

Warning and Disclaimer

This book is intended to offer information based on the author's research and experience regarding the material covered in this book. This book is sold with the agreement and understanding that the writer and/or the publisher are not engaged in providing any type of accounting, legal, or other professional advice. If legal representation or any other expert help is needed, the services of a skilled professional should be obtained.

In stocks, commodities, and mutual fund trading, there can be no guarantee of a profit. Losses can and do occur. As with any investment, you should carefully consider your suitability to trade and your ability to accept the financial risk of losing your entire investment. It should not be assumed that any indicator, method, or technique presented in this book will be profitable, or that it will not result in losses. Past performances are not necessarily indicative of future results. Examples in this book are for educational purposes only. This is not a solicitation of any order to buy or sell.

The information contained herein has been obtained from sources believed to be reliable, but cannot be guaranteed as to accuracy of entirety, and is subject to change without notice. There is a risk of loss trading futures and stocks. Using any trading method is the sole responsibility of the user.

CFTC DISCLAMER: "HYPOTHETICAL OR SIMULATED PERFORMANCE RESULTS HAVE CERTAIN INHERENT LIMITATIONS. UNLIKE AN ACTUAL PERFORMANCE RECORD SIMULATED RESULTS DO NOT REPRESENT ACTUAL TRADING. ALSO, SINCE THE TRADES HAVE NOT ACTUALLY BEEN EXECUTED, THE RESULTS MAY HAVE UNDER-OR-OVER COMPENSATED FOR THE IMPACT, IF ANY, OF CERTAIN MARKET FACTORS, SUCH AS LACK OF LIQUIDITY. SIMULATED TRADING PROGRAMS IN GENERAL ARE ALSO SUBJECT TO THE FACT THAT THEY ARE DESIGNED WITH THE BENEFIT OF HINDSIGHT. NO REPRESENTATION IS BEING MADE THAT ANY ACCOUNT WILL OR IS LIKELY TO ACHIEVE PROFITS OR LOSSES SIMILAR TO THOSE SHOWN."

The following notice applies whenever the names listed below are cited in this book.
TradeStation is a registered trademark of TradeStation, Inc. Kelly's Cycle Identifier is a trademark of ARC Systems, Inc. TrendPro is a trademark of ARC Systems, Inc.

TABLE OF CONTENTS

Chapter 3

Chapter 4

Chapter 5

Chapter 6

Chapter 7

Chapter 8

Chapter 9

Chapter 10

Innovative Methods Revealed

Chapter 11

Trading Patterns

Chapter 12

Identifying Trend

DEDICATION

I dedicate this book to my family for
all their help and support.

ACKNOWLEDGEMENTS

I would like to express my appreciation and thanks to all my clients and students for their encouragement and friendship; and special thanks to Debbie, Jenny and Brian for their proofreading and editing.

INTRODUCTION

*T*his book explains, in a comprehensive manner, a mechanical trading approach that I have found to be highly effective. It covers the application of trading any and all markets. In order to implement this mechanical strategy successfully, a considerable foundation and structured trading plan must first be put into place.

If you are a novice, there is information in Appendixes A-C that will help you get started. You will find information on charting programs, and other useful information.

As you make your way through this book, make a point of not getting stuck on any particular area or subject. If you find a particular subject difficult, I suggest temporarily skipping over it and returning to it later. As the old adage goes, "Don't Miss the Forest for the Trees." Additionally, after reading this book you may want to consider attending one of my seminars to complement the information you have attained.

It is not mandatory that my custom indicators be used in order to trade the methods referred to in this book. In Appendix B, you will find a conversion table that references indicators similar to the ones I use. However, it would be advantageous to use my custom indicators; the reason being is that they were designed and developed based upon my methods of trading.

CHAPTER 1

The Beginning

Laying a Good Foundation

*T*here are four main keys needed for a trader, or investor, to unlock the door to success in the market. The first key of importance is to acquire a good understanding of how the market works. The second would be to use good money management skills. The third is to have a good, proven trading method. The fourth is to understand the degree of importance that your personality plays in regards to trading. To succeed you must be able to recognize your *type* of personality, and be able to overcome any particular personality weaknesses that could cause you to lose money in the market.

There are basically two things that will hinder your success as a trader, and in return cause you to lose money—*Fear and Greed:* both of which are born out of the Lack of a Business Plan (trading plan). By understanding your personality, and working on any weaknesses you may have, you can overcome the *Fear and Greed* factor that can cause you, the trader, to lose money.

To help with the *Fear and Greed* aspect of trading, I have described three types of personalities, and most people will fall under one of these types. It is possible that you can relate to all three; however, for this self examination to really benefit you, you will need to identify the one that is predominantly recognizable in *your* personality.

The three personality types are: *Trigger-Happy Clyde, Slow Moe, and Ready Freddy.*

Trigger-Happy Clyde is the sort of individual that cannot find anything to his liking, nothing works well for Clyde. *Trigger-Happy Clydes* are very impatient and tend to buy all the latest and greatest stuff hoping to find a magic bullet. They always seem to be blaming their lack of trading skills on software, indicators, brokers, and/or their data feed, never coming to the realization that *they* are their own worst enemy.

Slow Moe is the person that has to know everything that can be known about anything. *Slow Moes* are very intelligent and very analytical. Prior to entering a trade, this kind of person requires a complete rundown on how their data vendors get the data, how the data in turn is sent to them, and how the programmer programmed the trading platform they are using to trade with. They need to know how each trading method works, and who came up with the method, etc., etc. When they think there is a trade, they keep waiting for more and more confirmation, and by the time they come up with all the reasons to enter the trade, the trade is over.

Ready Freddys have some weaknesses but have managed to overcome them as far as trading goes. *Ready Freddys* are quick to recognize their mistakes and they promptly correct them. This person has a trading plan and sticks with it, and does not let things get in the way of making trades. If *Ready Freddy* trades for a living, then he manages it like a business. Because *Ready Freddys* have done their homework, they are very confident in their ability and know what works the majority of the time. *Ready Freddys* understand that nothing works one hundred percent of the time; therefore, they use things that work the greater percentage of the time.

Slow Moes and *Trigger-Happy Clydes* can master their problems by using and staying with a good trading plan.

Let's now review some of the problems that all traders run into, and information on how to overcome these problems.

Dos and Don'ts of Trading

The Dos and Don'ts of Trading! What are they, and how can we keep from making the same mistakes as others?

Here are eight pitfalls that frequently cause a trader to lose money in the market: lack of a trading plan, lack of good money management, failure to use stops, taking very small profits, overstaying a position, overtrading your account, changing your trading strategy during market hours (especially when you're in a trade), and lack of patience.

Lack of a trading plan

Without a trading plan, a trader will not have a solid foundation; he will not have the building blocks needed to develop a clear understanding of how to make money trading. This is a common question you may hear from this type of trader, "A friend told me he heard bonds were going up, what do you think, should I buy?" He really doesn't know what to do, or if he does he doesn't have a plan in place to make it work.

Developing a trading plan is a MUST. Having a trading plan resolves many problems. Your trading plan does not need to be a complex set of rules; on the contrary, the less complicated your plan, the easier it will be to use. Although your plan does not need to be elaborate, it should address your entry, profit targets, and stops.

Lack of Money Management

There are as many opinions on money management as there are traders and investors. With that being said, what it boils down to is that each individual must decide for himself what type of money management he prefers to use. I will outline a few basic rules and ideas that will help.

Traders can avoid major losses by controlling their risk through stop losses. A trader should consider never risking more than 1% of his total equity on any one trade. By using this method, a trader can be wrong 20 times in a row and still leave 80% of his equity intact.

Another suggestion I make to traders is that if everything goes wrong, and they start having many losses in a row that result in a 25% loss of their investment, then they should stop trading for a period of time. Taking a break from trading for a few months will clear their head and give them time to reevaluate their trading plan and also analyze the trades that were taken in order to determine the problem. Only after the problem is found and resolved should an individual start trading again.

If a trader has a 50/50 win/loss ratio, and the wins are greater than the losses, then that trader would be making money. Based on the track records you keep, you will gain insight into how many trades will become winners and how many will become losers.

Using good money management includes not giving up more than a fixed percentage of your account on any one trade; and in my opinion, it also includes controlling your risk on each trade by using a stop and a profit target. This part of your trading plan will be the decisive factor that determines whether or not you will become a successful trader.

Failure to use stops

This is when the trader has no fixed stop in the pit (or has not placed one electronically). This does not mean a mental stop; but rather a stop loss order in the pit. There are many problems with a mental stop. First of all, it is too easy to keep changing it in your mind. Next is the probability of not being able to call your broker in time. Additionally, if you are trading electronically, there is the possibility of your internet connection going down—any one of these things could possibly prevent you from placing the stop in time.

You should always calculate your stop, and be sure to place the stop after you have entered the trade. If you are placing your trades over the internet, there are many trading platforms that will automatically place the stop and the profit target at the same time the trade is entered. Once in a trade, the stop and target can usually be easily adjusted if needed.

Taking very small profits

One very common mistake is jumping out of a trade with very little profit and letting the losers run. The trader becomes impatient, and rather than staying with the trade until completion (reaching the profit target or getting stopped out), he jumps out early ending up with a small (if any) profit, or possibly a small loss.

To prevent this, you need to develop a trading method that works the greater percentage of the time, and Stick to it! This helps build your confidence, and confidence is what you need to combat the Fear and Greed factor from taking control.

The saying "You never go broke taking a profit" is in my opinion the most worthless advice ever given to a trader. Taking small profits will eat up your account very fast. This is because when the market goes against you, and you have a bad trade, it usually takes many good trades to offset the one losing trade. This means the win/loss ratio would have to be approximately 90/10 and even the best of the best could never maintain such a high percentage of winning trades. The real money in trading comes from winning trades being larger than losing trades, and having more winning trades than losing trades. The trader needs to develop the skill and attitude to stay with trades based on good trading rules that have been proven over time to produce profits.

Overstaying your position

Staying in a trade too long is caused from not using a profit target. The trader may be thinking, "There is more money to be made, so why not let it run."

You can eliminate this trap by sticking to your trading plan, which includes your profit target. Rather than giving in to spur-of-the-moment emotions, focus on *not* deviating from your plan.

If you want more out of a trade, and want to let it run, I would recommend using a trailing stop. However, all the testing I have personally done with trailing stops has not proven any more profitable than using a fixed profit target.

Overtrading your account

Overtrading your account can happen by losing too much of your account on any given trade, and/or giving up a major portion of your account before you get a handle on what is causing your losses. Before this happens to you, take a step back, identify the problem, and correct it. Then, and only then, resume trading.

Should the market go against you, you must have a fixed percentage you are willing to give up. Never use funds that are needed for yourself or your family's support.

Changing your strategy during market hours or during a trade

This is a very common mistake. This happens when there are no set of rules and/or no trading plan.

A trader needs to establish a set of rules and stay with them when in a trade. Of course, these need to be proven rules that have been tested and that work the greater percentage of the time.

Lack of patience

The average life span of a commodity or stock trader can be very short-lived, and this is generally the fault of the trader himself. Having a good set of rules will greatly increase your odds of survival. Many trade just because they like the action. You should never force a trade; in other words, do not create one just to be trading. Be careful of illusions, such as manufacturing a trade in your mind because you think one should be there.

Be patient: Do not chase the market. Let the market come to you; meaning, you wait for a trade setup to occur based on your trading plan. In some markets this may take days—even on a five minute chart. If you should miss a trade, wait for a new setup to occur before re-entering. Once a trade is entered, allow enough time for the trade to develop and give it enough time to reach your profit target or stop.

However, by knowing that your profit targets are larger than your stops (meaning your winning trades will be larger than your losing trades), along with the knowledge that your winning trades outnumber your losing trades, getting stopped out should no longer be a concern.

Developing a Trading Plan

Most traders put all their focus into *when* and *where* to get into a trade. That's only part of it; the other part is good money management. Traders are forever searching for the Holy Grail—money management is the Holy Grail—they just refuse to see it. In order to be in control of your trading, you should never neglect the money management aspect of your trading plan.

Outlining a plan for successful trading

- When & Where to enter a trade

- Where to take profits

- Where to place stops

A well-developed trading plan will take the *Fear and Greed* out of trading. This is the same *Fear and Greed* that is responsible for causing most traders to lose money.

Many traders ask me, "Can I get a copy of your trading plan?" My answer to that is, "It wouldn't do you any good to try and use my trading plan, as it is custom-designed for me." Each trader has to make his own individualized plan based on his risk capital and emotional makeup.

A very basic trading plan may look something like this:

- I will only trade in the direction of the trend.

- I will use trend lines and major cycles to determine the direction of the trend.

- I will use a moving average crossover to enter a trade.

- I will use a fixed stop of two points.

- I will use a fixed profit target of six points.

- I will never break my rules during a trade.

Three Steps for successful trading:

- Trade in the direction of the trend.

- Buy if the market is trending up.

- Sell if the market is trending down.

"Everyone knows to trade in the direction of the trend, unfortunately very few follow it. The ones who do will become winners." *Roy Kelly*

A familiar statement is, "The trend is your friend." "Trade in the direction of the market" is another way to put this. Another familiar statement is "Easier said than done!" Later we will cover how to define trend direction and trend reversals.

There are many factors that a trader needs to take into consideration in order to be able to put together a successful trading plan. Here are a few questions to consider: Do I only take long positions, *or* do I only take short positions? Or do I take short *and* long positions? How do I identify the trend and trend reversals? What qualifications need to be met to enter a trade, and where do I place my profit targets and stops?

Every trader will have a unique set of rules. These rules will vary depending on each individual's risk capital, anxiety level, and what is being traded. Throughout this book I will show some methods that will help eliminate negative emotions and help the reader become a better trader. By deductive reasoning one can eliminate the impossible, and what is left is the possible! Therefore, the logical conclusion is for us to eliminate what doesn't work and concentrate on what is left.

So far the information that has been presented may seem elementary, and therefore, easily disregarded. However, I have found that ignoring the most basic rules is the cause for many, if not most, traders to become ex-traders. Two of the most basic rules often ignored include not having a trading plan that works, and/or the lack of good money management skills.

I repeat for emphasis—there are two main things that cause a trader to lose money, *Fear and Greed*. To keep these two things in check, do not dismiss these two rules: Have a trading plan that works and apply good money management.

There is no real genius in any of these rules or suggestions; they are only common sense and nothing else. Common sense is a must in order to become, and remain, a successful trader. When we trade opposite to common sense we will, of course, lose. If a trader lacks (or ignores) common sense, losses will be inevitable. This may not happen right away or all the time; however, trading against the direction of the market isn't using common sense and can only spell disaster for the trader.

CHAPTER 2

The Evolution of Theories

From Dow to Now

*B*efore the advent of the Stock Exchange, stocks were traded through brokers at coffeehouses and on the roadside. These traders had never even heard of a Starbucks or a laptop computer. Trading under a buttonwood tree at 68 Wall Street led to the formation of the New York Stock Exchange. Today the term "Wall Street" frequently refers to the financial markets worldwide with a stock market open somewhere at any given time on any given day.

Today, with the world seemingly spinning faster and faster, you may at times feel that trading is very difficult—and it can be. Maybe one of the reasons that it can become overwhelming is because there is so much information available. Consider the Greats of Old. All they had was a ticker tape, or some type of written report they received at the end of the day. Going back in time before the computer age, the only thing investors had to go on was the closing price of the markets they were trading. There was no high, low, or open—only the closing price. And most of their work was done by hand, even drawing the charts and calculating out the indicators. Every trader today has a great deal more to work with. With one click on a computer mouse, or a few keystrokes on the computer keyboard, we can add an indicator, view live charts, and even place a trade electronically through the internet. This chapter is dedicated to the Greats of Old who paved the way to where we are today. *All progress is due to those who were not satisfied to let well enough alone --Unknown.*

As you go through the rest of this chapter, you will be reading about different theories that were developed by a diverse group of innovative individuals over a sizeable span of time. As a result, each of these distinct theories concerning the stock market contains various terms used by the originator of that particular theory. It is understandable, and potentially confusing, that this diversity would result in an inconsistency regarding the meaning of various terms. Therefore, it would be good to keep in mind that the terminology used by one individual can be used to mean something entirely different by another. Discernment is needed to ascertain what each writer is referring to as you examine that particular individual's work. In other words, by understanding that there is no official terminology used in the trading world, we are able to focus on the overall concepts being conveyed.

The brief synopses of the following individuals are not arranged in any particular order. They each had their own unique perspectives and theories to add to the overall analysis of the stock market.

Fibonacci Analysis

Fibonacci, or perhaps more correctly, Leonardo Pisano, was born in the year 1170 and died in 1250. Fibonacci was born in Italy, but received his education in North Africa where his father, Guilielmo Bonacci, worked in a diplomatic capacity representing the merchants of the Republic of Pisa who were trading in Bugia (later named Bougie and currently known as Bejaia). Fi'-Bonacci is short for Filius Bonacci, which in Latin means "the son of Bonacci." Fibonacci originated the numerical sequence known as the Fibonacci sequence after a trip to Egypt sometime in the thirteenth century.

Later, men like Ralph Elliott applied these numbers to the stock market. The Fibonacci series of numbers are: 1-1-2-3-5-8-13-21… Every number in this series is equivalent to the two preceding numbers, and in several places in nature, these ratios have been observed. The most common way for a trader to use Fibonacci numbers is to identify a major turn point, then from the major turn point project Fibonacci support and resistance areas; however, they can be calculated from any degree of a turn point.

I, and others, have added more to the research and development of using Fibonacci numbers with the market. In my opinion, Fibonacci numbers can help in some areas of trading; for instance, support and resistance levels. As with any theory, caution is always warranted. It's just like my friend, a trader, once said, "If you put enough lines on the chart, the market will turn off one of them." Some people simply refer to Fibonacci numbers as Fib numbers.

Some traders feel that it is important to use Fibonacci numbers in all aspects of their trading. They base the time frame they are trading by Fibonacci numbers. They also use the Fibonacci numbers for their indicators, like a moving average. For instance, if the moving average came with a default setting of 9, they would prefer to use a Fibonacci number like 8 or 13. There are many other ways to use Fibonacci numbers in trading. More information on Fibonacci Extensions and Fibonacci Support & Resistance levels will be included throughout the book (these are the two Fibonacci tools that I prefer). As with the Elliott Waves, Fibonacci numbers can tie up much time and research. If a trader, i.e. *Slow Moe*, tried to incorporate all of the applications in the following list, I believe he would spend an extraordinary amount of time doing research and very little time trading—*if any*.

The following Fibonacci applications are very interesting and have certain benefits. However, from my experience and research, I believe that the amount of time and concentration required to absorb the information greatly takes away from the value of their use.

- Fibonacci Bands

- Fibonacci Ovals

- Fibonacci Arcs

- Fibonacci Spirals

- Fibonacci Trend Lines

- Fibonacci Expansions

- Fibonacci Price & Time

Dow Theory

Charles H. Dow (1851-1902) was the editor and founder of the *Wall Street Journal*, and founder of the *Dow Jones News Service*. Dow was the author of many editorials about the stock market. These editorials became the basis for the Dow Theory. His work has endured the test of time. Today the understanding of his work is providing a lucrative living for many traders.

From his observations of the stock market, Dow came up with three types of movement to establish trend. The primary trend is first, which can take place over a period of years (it can either be a bullish or a bearish trend). The secondary movement is next and can take place anywhere from a few weeks to several months. These secondary movements can turn against the main direction of the primary trend. The third type of movement is a day-to-day fluctuation that can move in either direction, bullish or bearish. The day-to-day fluctuations are of small importance (other than that they make up the overall trend). Dow's theory can be applied to position trading as well as day trading.

The importance of understanding this method becomes clear when used to establish the direction of the trend. When the price breaks through a preceding high or low turn point, the trend can then be established. Intermediate (secondary) high and low turn points are useful only for short term trends. Major high and low turn points are essential for identifying major trends.

On the following page is a layout that shows Dow's basic theory.

Dow's Basic Theory

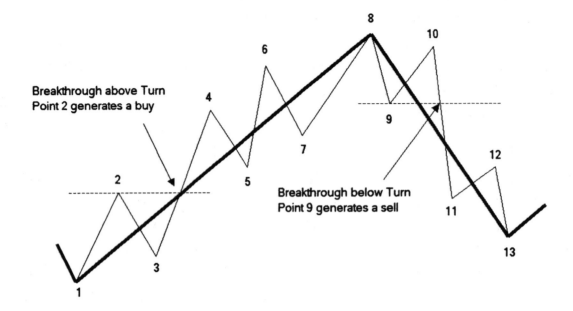

This graph is showing Dow's primary trend and secondary trend. The primary trend would be 1, 8, and 13. The secondary trend would be the intermediate trend identified by turn points 2, 3, 4, 5, 6, 7, 9, 10, 11, 12. Keep in mind that during the time of Dow's works in the field of market analysis, day trading (as we know it today) did not exist.

How Dow describes an uptrend is when consecutive rallies in a security price close at levels higher than those in previous rallies, and when lows happen at levels higher than previous lows. Downtrends happen when the markets make lower lows and lower highs. It is this hypothesis of the Dow Theory that provides the basis for the principle defined as price trend. Dow described what he saw as a recurring theme in the markets. Price would move sharply in one direction, retrace shortly in the reverse direction, and then continue in the original direction.

Gann Theory

William D. Gann (1878-1955) stated, "Speculation or investment can be the 'best' business in the world if you make a 'real' business of it. But in order to make a success at it you must study, be prepared— and you must not guess, follow inside information, or depend on hope/fear. If you do you will fail. Your trading success depends on knowing the right kind of rules and following them." Gann had the ability to forecast price movements in the market. He also had an ability to increase money at an incredible rate, even by today's standards.

His work was innovative, but is difficult to use on most intraday time charts, and even for position trading, it is very time-consuming. Gann spent more than ten years in other countries, including England and Egypt, where he studied in their libraries. He reviewed and studied a wide variety of subject matters, including anything he could find on natural law, and the cycles in nature and in the universe. Incorporating his findings on definite numbers that occur throughout all religious and obscure documents, Gann came up with some amazing approaches to trading the stock market. His approach to the stock market was very complex and considerable time is needed to understand all of his work. I will not cover his work in this book, as it would take a master set of volumes to do so.

It was interesting reading for me when I read some of Gann's quotes from *The Ticker and Investment Digest*. It reminded me of the things I discovered on my own quest for finding success as a trader. Previous to writing this chapter I had not researched his work; however, in doing so I found some quotes of his that you will no doubt find as interesting as I did. Here are some of Gann's quotes which I found of interest taken from *The Ticker and Investment Digest*, Vol. 5, No. 2, December 1909.

"For the past ten years I have devoted my entire time and attention to the speculative markets. Like many others, I lost thousands of dollars and experienced the usual ups and downs incidental to the novice who enters the market without preparatory knowledge of the subject."

--William D. Gann

"I soon began to realize that all successful men, whether lawyers, doctors, or scientists, devoted years of time to the study and investigation of their particular pursuit or profession before attempting to make any money out of it."

--William D. Gann

"Being in the brokerage business myself and handling large accounts, I had opportunities seldom afforded the ordinary man for studying the cause of success and failure in the speculations of others. I found that over ninety percent of the traders who go into the market without knowledge or study usually lose in the end."

--William D. Gann

Notice what Gann said comes *before* success, "I lost thousands of dollars." Then in his next quote he said, "I soon began to realize that all successful men…devoted years of time to the study and investigation of their particular pursuit or profession before attempting to make any money out of it."

Much of what Gann observed is still commonplace today in the trading arena. One outstanding truth is that most (if not all) successful traders have a similar story of losing money before they were willing to invest the needed time and effort into study and research, which then led to their success. Perhaps there is a lesson to be learned here by those who have not yet fallen into this unfortunate circumstance!

Elliott Wave Theory

Ralph Nelson Elliott (1871-1948) developed some stimulating ideas in regard to price action in the stock market, and his ideas will continue to influence the way investors on Wall Street view the stock market for years to come. Elliott was somewhat vague in his qualifications for waves of numerous magnitudes, and his followers will disagree on different turn points. Filtering the magnitude of the degree of the wave is helpful in identifying the tradable waves.

Ralph Elliott was an accountant who lived in South America for many years. Later, in 1927, he moved to Los Angeles where he retired and developed the Elliott Wave Theory. The Wave Theories were published in monograph in 1938 and called *The Wave Principle*. *The Wave Principle* was covered in 1939 by *Financial World Publication* in a series of different articles, and was also published again in 1946 in a book called *Nature's Law*. Elliott's Wave Principle was so interesting to stock investors that it prompted him to move to New York, and there he continued to write financial reports until his death.

Elliott essentially believed that the market prices varied in natural ways. In essence, he based his thoughts on the series of Fibonacci numbers: 1-1-2-3-5-8-13-21… Every one of the numbers in this series is equivalent in value to the two previous numbers, and in numerous areas in nature, these ratios have been discovered. Elliott established that Fibonacci numbers often exist in the stock market and also in the timing of the waves.

In addition to his fundamental conclusions, Elliott listed numerous variations. Elliott used the high and low prices rather than the closing prices. Elliott said, "In fact it was only with the establishment of the daily range in 1928 and the hourly averages in 1932 that sufficient reliable data became available to establish the rhythmic recurrence of the phenomenon called the *Wave Principle*." According to comments made by Elliott, the news has very little impact on the sequence of his wave series. He stated that the news media might affect the amplification of the price and time of the waves, but not the series itself. He also felt that the price usually moves inside channels. These channels can be effective in the interpretation of waves. The different degrees of waves that he used are listed below:

- Subminuette (used only for intraday times)
- Minuette
- Minor
- Intermediate
- Primary
- Cycle
- Super Cycle
- Grand Super Cycle

There are also many variations to his basic pattern. Elliott established five types of corrections. Listed below are the names of the variations and corrections:

- Triangles
- Irregular
- Flats
- Complex
- Zigzag

In order for a trader to become familiar with Elliot's method, he must be willing to invest a considerable amount of time into research. Also, it is almost impossible to day trade with it on short time frames (intraday).

For the most part, intraday time frames move too fast. Based on what I have seen, if you took one hundred devotees of the Elliott Wave Theory and gave them the same charts, each one would figure the Elliott Wave pattern differently.

Elliott's Basic Wave

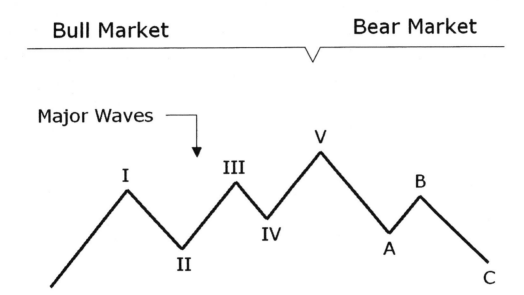

Gartley Theory

Harold M. Gartley, 1899-1972, has long been known as one of the all-time greats in the stock market. He started out being a board boy and runner on Wall Street. Gartley wrote many articles on the stock market, but he is best known for his book *Profits in the Stock Market*. He evolved into a master technician, whose techniques on trading the market are still in use today. He was an advocate for the Charles Dow Theory, and in his book he references it a few times. Gartley was a big believer in trend lines, using them with various strengths, and as trend channels. He had this to say about trend lines, "A study of trend lines over many years shows that this working tool does not give uniformly accurate indications. It must be used as one of several aids which help the technical student to reduce guesswork as far as possible."

You will find that among many of the most advanced traders today, his work remains a part of their trading strategies. The most commonly used pattern is referred to as the "Gartley," which is a complex Fibonacci pattern.

Gartley Bullish Pattern

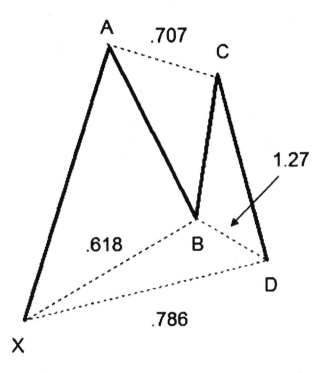

The formula to calculate this is: AB should be 61.8% of XA, BC should be 61.8-78.6% of AB, CD should be 127-161.8% of BC, and AD should be 78.6% of XA. The long entry point would occur at D (it would be wise to use other indicators to help confirm D as a buy point).

Gartley Bearish Pattern

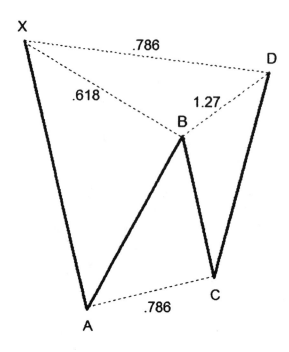

The formula to calculate this is: AB should be 61.8% of XA, BC should be 61.8-78.6% of AB, CD should be 127-161.8% of BC, and AD should be 78.6% of XA. The short entry point would occur at D (it would be wise to use other indicators to help confirm D as a sell point).

Kelly Theory

Roy Kelly, professional trader, lecturer, and author, began investing in the stock market in the middle 1970s. Upon realizing the huge potential that trading had to offer, he became a serious student of the stock market. Later, he began developing his own indicators and methods of trading, which eventually led to the sharing of his methods in the markets by conducting educational seminars and internet discussion groups. Some of the more widely used works, besides his trading methods, are his proprietary custom-designed indicators: Kelly's Cycle Identifier, Kelly's Advanced Moving Average, and many more.

The essence of his theory is that a trend reversal can be discovered when the price of the next turn point holds above or below the previous turn point. The current turn point needs to have more of a degree of movement than the previous turn point before it, and the predetermined movement in price from the current turn point needs to be confirmed before the trade is entered. It helps to have trend line(s) and/or Fibonacci support at the current price.

Presently residing in the USA, Roy continues to be a leader in the business. Over his career as a trader and software developer Roy has had the pleasure of being both publicly and privately acknowledged as such by both his colleagues and the trading community as a whole. One such recognition came from the 1997 April/May issue of *Futures Truth Magazine* which listed his system #1 with a remarkable above average rate of return. More recently Roy was honored with what many consider to be the most prestigious of awards in the trading software industry—*TradeStation's 1st place Community Choice Award* for favorite add-on indicators for his *Floor Traders Tools* software. Roy continues to enjoy traveling the country presenting his "Trade Like the Pros" seminars several times a year.

Kelly's Basic Theory

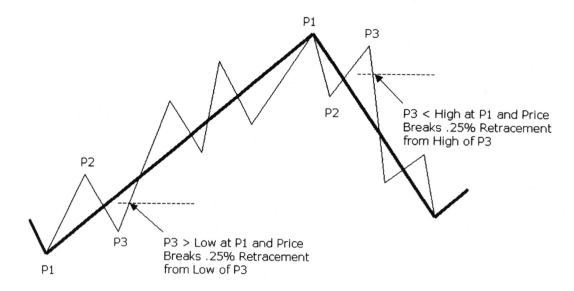

P1

P3

P2

P3 < High at P1 and Price
Breaks .25% Retracement
from High of P3

P2

P3

P3 > Low at P1 and Price
Breaks .25% Retracement
from Low of P3

P1

In his theory he recognizes three turn points, the major being the dominant turn point, the intermediate being the trading turn point, and the minor turn point. He feels there is very little use for the minor turn points, as they do not usually have enough price movement to be tradable. He uses the intermediate turn points for entry and trend reversals, and the major turn points for direction and longer term trading (position trading).

For the sake of practicality, he only uses two cycles in his trading method: major cycles and intermediate cycles.

The chapters that follow are intended to help you cut down on your research, thereby saving you time. Nevertheless, you must not neglect developing a solid trading plan of your own.

CHAPTER 3

Trading Indicators

Indicators and Price

*I*t may be of a surprise to some that indicators can only work with the information received from the data vendor (from the charting program you are using). Usually what is transmitted is limited to time, volume, open, high, low, and close. What this translates into is, all indicators work off this information and most indicators only work off the closing price. Few indicators use the open, high, or low price, and very few use time, or volume.

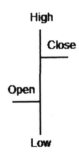

Leading Indicators

A leading indicator is used to help forecast which direction the market may be headed. Some of these indicators are: support and resistance, trend line extensions, Kelly's Cycle Forecaster, and

Fibonacci levels. I have done a lot of research on leading indicators and have found that they can serve as very useful tools. The ones that I have found to be the most helpful with my trading are: support and resistance, Fibonacci retracements, and cycle forecasting.

More recently traders have been putting a lot of trust in Fibonacci confluence areas. This is where multiple Fibonacci numbers from different time frames merge together. In my research, I still find more value in the age-old floor pivots for support and resistance.

Lagging Indicators

Lagging indicators require price action before the indicators turn. They confirm price action and move with the price. In other words, they lag behind the market. They are still very useful, and can help in trading. Some lagging indicators are: RSI, moving averages, and stochastic, to name a few. Some refer to lagging indicators as confirming indicators. I feel that the best of both leading and lagging indicators should be used. Combining leading and lagging indicators works well for analyzing a chart.

There are different terms for indicators, and there are many indicators that are very similar but have different names, depending on who last modified them. An example of this is the many different variations of oscillators, a.k.a. overbought and oversold indicators—one such indicator being the stochastic. Others have improved certain oscillators by smoothing them out to be more adaptable to market conditions.

Here is a list of a few stochastics:

- Fast Stochastic
- Slow Stochastic
- Raw Stochastic
- Modified Stochastic
- The Stochastic
- Double Stochastic
- Smooth Stochastic
- Dual Stochastic
- Two Smooth

Some traders find oscillators difficult to use. This is because they have the opinion that in really trendy markets oscillators tend to get stuck in an overbought or oversold position. One way to address this problem would be to determine if the market is trading in a range, in which case an oscillator usually works well. However, if the market is trending you would need something in addition to oscillators to help show direction such as trend lines, support and resistance levels, or moving averages.

At the time oscillators were developed, they worked well; however, markets today have more of a directional trend, and less amplitude between swings, making the oscillators somewhat difficult to use. Many traders still incorporate oscillators into their trading plan, and there are currently some oscillators available which have been customized to better adapt to current market conditions. I prefer to use oscillators mainly for showing divergence. Divergence is covered in *Chapter 4, Trading Methods*. For showing trend I personally like to use something that is more adapted to market conditions. *Chapter 12, Identifying Trend,* will provide further clarification on this subject.

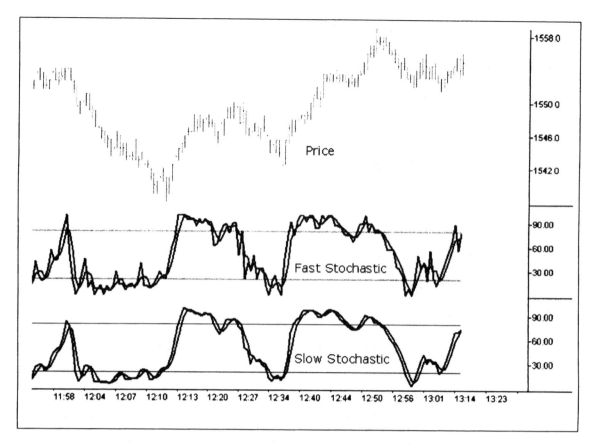

The difference between the fast stochastic and slow stochastic is that the fast stochastic has more noise (false signals—or as some would say—faster signals) than the slow stochastic. There are many standard ones that come with charting programs. Some developers have designed stochastics that perform better than the standard ones that come with charting programs. My Two Smooth stochastic shown on the next page is one such stochastic.

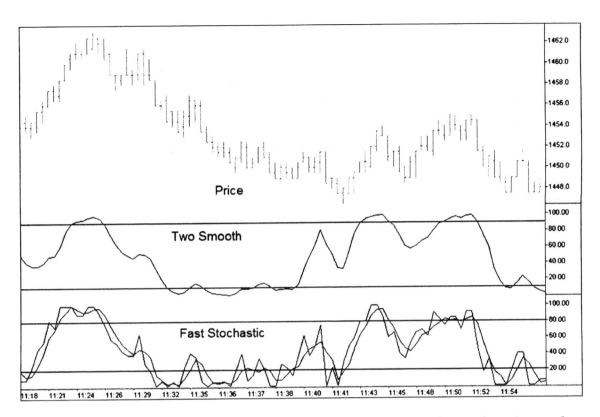

This chart shows the difference between a normal stochastic and a custom-designed one (Two Smooth). As you can see, there is far less noise in the custom stochastic.

Moving Averages

There are many different types of moving averages. Some moving averages are very useful, and like the stochastic, there are many of them. From the first few basic ones have come many—and even these offshoots have been modified by individuals, making them better than the default ones that come standard with most charting programs.

Here is a list of some of the moving averages:

- Moving Average
- Adaptive Moving Average
- Exponential Moving Average
- Triangular Moving Average
- Weighted Moving Average
- Displaced Moving Average
- Kelly's Advanced Moving Average

I have found two moving averages that work reasonably well—exponential moving average and my Kelly's Advanced Moving Average. You can plot the Kelly's Advanced Moving Average over the price and use it just like you would any other moving average. The exponential moving average works well with the correct setting for showing overall direction of the trend. Using two of them (one with a length of 27 and the other with a length of 50) works well in most markets. Further in the book, I will illustrate how I use these different indicators.

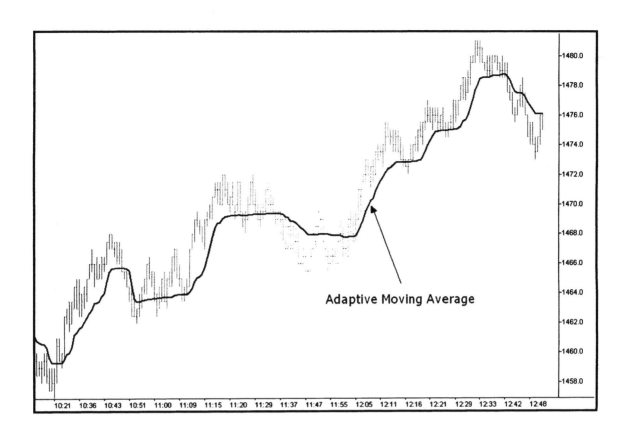

Adaptive Moving Average

This chart shows an adaptive moving average. The chart on the following page will show an exponential moving average.

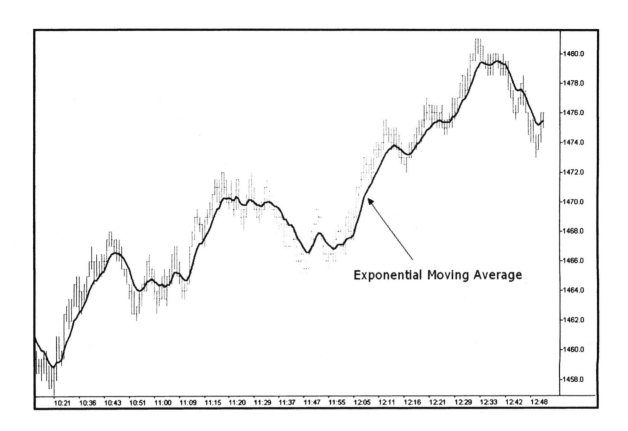

Exponential Moving Average

The above chart shows an exponential moving average.

The chart on the next page shows various moving averages to illustrate the differences among a few of them. These are shown with standard default settings, but you can change many of the settings in each indicator to your preference.

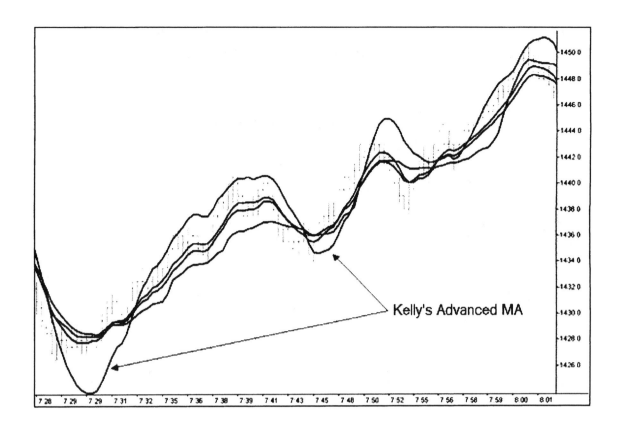

Kelly's Advanced MA

There are four moving averages on this chart: adaptive moving average, exponential moving average, weighted moving average, and the Kelly's Advanced Moving Average. As seen here, there is very little difference between them, with the exception of the Kelly's Advanced Moving Average.

I prefer my Kelly's Advanced Moving Average because it swings above and below the price at cycle tops and cycle bottoms, thereby showing more of a dramatic move in the indicator (notice how it cups the price and will start to lead the price). An input setting that works well would be a length between 19 and 27, depending on the market.

From the basic moving averages came a host of other indicators like the MACD (Moving Average Convergence Divergence).

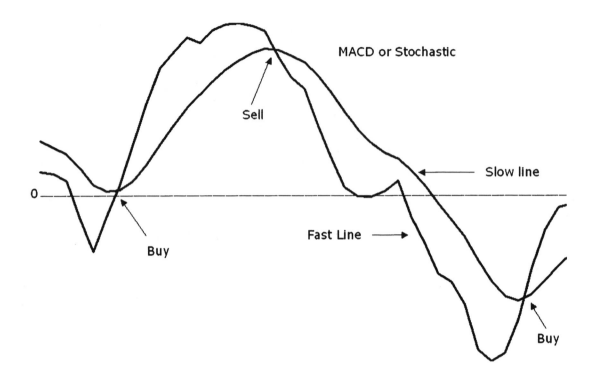

The above chart shows how most traders buy and sell based on the MACD, or stochastic. Caution is needed because you cannot make money by taking every trade based on the crossover of the oscillator. More technical analysis is necessary to identify the tradable cycles. On the next page is a review of stronger and weaker signals in oscillators.

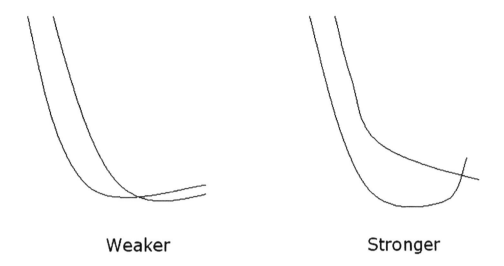

Weaker   Stronger

Whipsaw is when the market starts to reverse, and then whips the other way against the direction expected. The market moves up just enough to get the majority of traders in a long position, and then goes the other way. When the price whipsaws, and goes in the opposite direction, the price will usually move very quickly. This illustration is showing that by waiting for the stronger moves (rather than trying to trade the weaker ones), you can avoid whipsaws.

Knowledge of available trading indicators will carry you only so far. To be a survivor and be among the profitable traders, you need to apply methods different than those being used by everyone else. By doing this, you will not be among those who lose money trading. If it were as simple as buying and selling an overbought or oversold oscillator when it crosses over, then you would need to ask yourself, "Where do all the losses come from, and why do so many people lose money on their trading investments?" It's because they are applying methods that don't work, and because of poor money management. The solution—master methods and money management skills that others don't possess. This requires study, research, and testing the methods *before* trading.

CHAPTER 4

Trading Methods

···

Understanding Different Trading Methods

*T*here are basically two styles of trading: Non-Judgmental and Judgmental. Non-Judgmental traders employ a mechanical approach to trading. This approach uses a trading plan that a trader sticks to religiously, as was discussed in Chapter 1.

Judgmental traders, on the other hand, base their decisions largely on sentiment. They are more apt to take risks; which in turn, require structure and a larger brokerage account. There are some inherent problems with Judgmental trading—the trader will most likely lack discipline, and make decisions hastily based on news reports and/or other factors that may influence the human mind. This approach requires the trader to make decisions depending on any given situation. Judgmental trading is difficult, requiring good concentration, and self-discipline. I have heard that there are traders out there who make money using a Judgmental approach; however, it is my opinion that they are more than likely destined for failure. In the thirty plus years that I have been in the business, I have not met many Judgmental traders that have been successful. That is not to say that a trader cannot trade with a method that incorporates using his judgment; however, I would highly recommend a good set of trading rules to go along with it, and in that trading plan allow for making a judgment call.

I do not recommend the Judgmental approach; however, if you prefer this method of trading, be sure to make it a part of your trading plan. It would also be a good idea to keep track of the number of times your judgment helped your trading versus the number of times it hindered it. By doing so, you will be able to look back on your trades and determine what percentage of the time your judgment helped in making a profitable trade. If your judgment calls did not help with making profitable trades at least sixty percent of the time, I would recommend eliminating them from your trading plan.

The style in which you trade will depend on *your* account size and *your* emotional makeup. You are the only one who can decide how you will trade.

By now you should have a firm understanding of the important role that being a knowledgeable trader plays, and what kind of things can cause a trader to either succeed or fail. Keep in mind that if the market goes against you with no stops in place, it can wipe out in just one day what took a week or more to make.

Remember that *Fear and Greed* are the two biggest obstacles that cause traders to lose money. Having a trading plan eliminates the *Fear and Greed* factor and puts structure into one's trading. When you disregard your Trading Plan, that's when mistakes will happen.

There are many different theories about trading. In the following pages I will review some of them. One thing that I take into consideration is the percentage of accuracy of an indicator (or method) I am using before I implement it into my trading plan. I will only use it if it proves to be accurate a good majority of the time (in the vicinity of sixty-five percent).

At my seminars I often ask this question to the attendees, "How many know what your percentage of winning trades is?" The response reveals that only about twenty percent of them have taken the time to keep a record of their trades. This is the foundation that a trader should build from. If one doesn't have a solid foundation, then how can one build on it? A trader needs to be able to recognize and change whatever is hindering his success as a trader, and money management is critical in this regard.

I cannot emphasize enough how important money management is in regards to your success in this business, and that includes knowing your percentage of winning trades. Under Appendix C there is a basic layout for keeping a track record.

Understanding Theories and Terms

There are many different terms used in trading—cycles and turn points are among them. Cycles can be referred to as turn points, cycle points, wave points, peaks and valleys, and swing points. Be careful not to mix up turn points with swing points—there is a difference and I will cover that subject in more detail in the next two chapters. Note that all swing points are not tradable turn points.

Traders have labeled turn points as A, B, C; cycle 1, cycle 2, cycle 3; wave 1, wave 2, wave 3; turn point 1, turn point 2, turn point 3; and P1, P2, P3. Really they are all the same; only the names have been changed to protect the innocent. For the most part, I will use A, B and C, or P1, P2, and P3 when making any reference to turn points on a chart. Turn points must have a big enough move in price to be, in my opinion, considered tradable turn points. I will be covering this in more detail further on.

Chart Patterns

There are many different price patterns, and these price patterns come in many forms and with many different names. Here are a few of the names that are used:

- Coils
- Under Hits
- Pennants
- Gartley
- Double Top
- Double Bottom
- Triple Top
- Triple Bottom
- Head & Shoulders
- And many more

Several of the above patterns will be reviewed throughout later chapters. The two following pages will illustrate a few of these price patterns.

Head & Shoulders Pattern

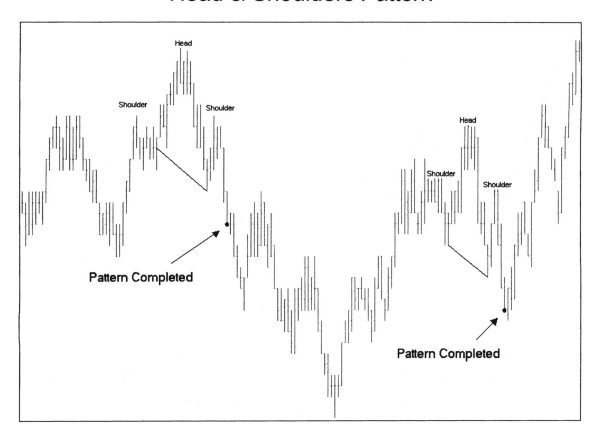

The above chart shows two typical Head & Shoulders patterns. Caution is needed when taking a position based on this pattern alone. Often times, after the pattern is completed, the market will reverse and go in the other direction. The Head & Shoulders pattern on the left demonstrates one that would have been profitable. The pattern on the right shows that the market has whipsawed in the other direction.

Double Bottom & Double Top Pattern

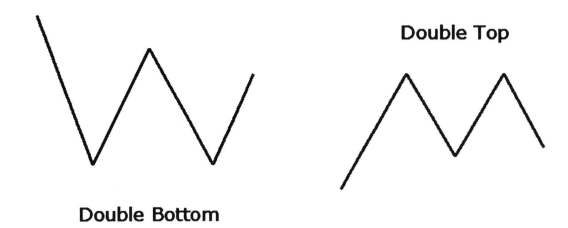

Double Top

Double Bottom

Seen here on the left is a depiction of a normal double bottom pattern; and on the right is a normal double top pattern. There are also triple bottom patterns, and triple top patterns.

Trend Lines

Trend lines are drawn through swing points. A trend line drawn through minor swing points can be extended a short way; trend lines drawn through intermediate turn points can be projected further into the future. Trend lines are useful for support and resistance. They can also be used to show breakout and trend reversals.

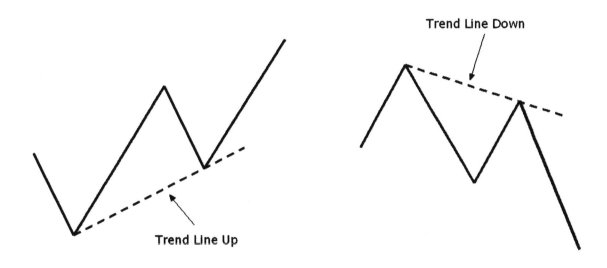

The trend lines in the above graph show support and resistance and then, in most cases, are extended to the right to show the next support or resistance. The trend line up is drawn from a swing point low to the next swing point low. The trend line down is drawn from a swing point high to the next swing point high.

Trend Line Breakouts

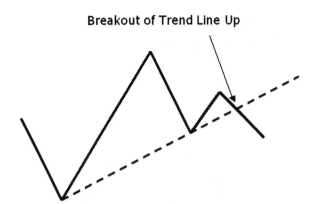

As seen in the above graph, trend lines can help show the direction of the trend and trend reversals on a price breakout of the trend line. The chart on the following page shows a reversal that is often referred to as a triangle breakout failure.

Triangle Breakout Failure

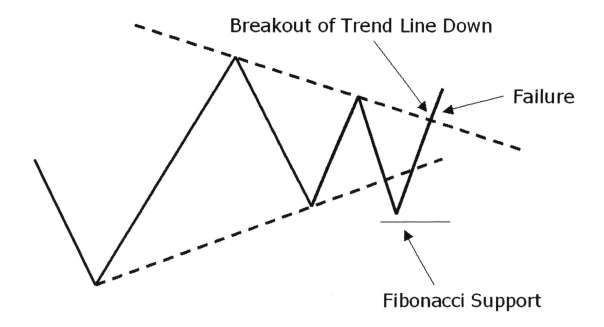

This pattern is often found on intraday time charts. The triangle breakout failure can materialize in many different forms. The strategy is for the trader to establish that the triangle does exist, be able to see it form, and then be able to act upon it either by exiting (closing) their position if short, or reversing their position. In the example above, a triangle breakout failure needs the close of a price bar to be greater than the trend line down to qualify as a triangle breakout.

Triangle Breakout Failure

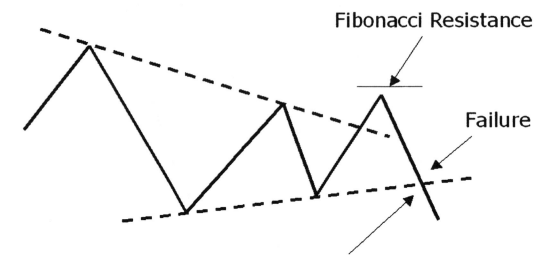

Fibonacci Resistance

Failure

Breakout of Trend Line Up

The graph above shows a breakout to the upside that failed at a Fibonacci resistance area. It then breaks down through the trend line up—and that's where the failure occurs and the price reverses.

Trend Line Channels

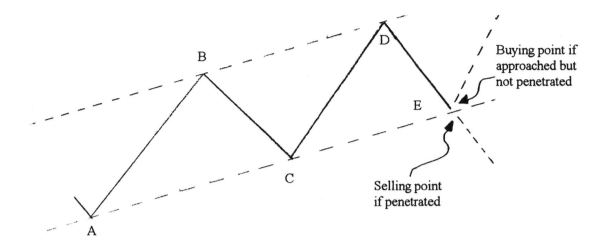

This hand-drawn illustration shows the use of two trend lines, below and above the turn points. If the price pivots above the lower trend line, that would be an area for buying. However, if the price breaks below the lower trend line, it would trigger a short entry. Of course, it would be prudent to use other indicators to confirm the long or short entry.

Divergence

There are several indicators that help in determining when the market is going to reverse, and divergence is one key factor in determining when a market may be reversing. There are many different oscillators that will show divergence. RSI (Relative Strength Index), Stochastic, MACD (Moving Average Convergence), and others can be used.

Bullish Divergence

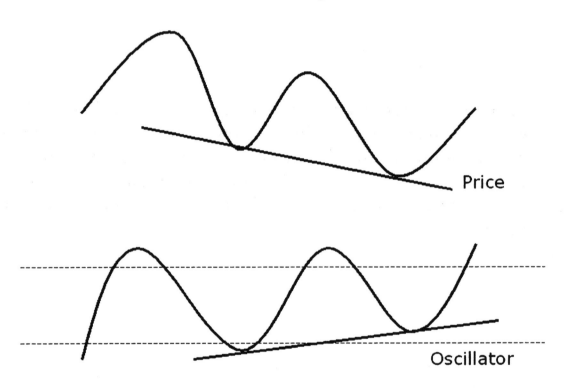

The graph above is showing bullish Divergence, and I added trend lines for clearer identification. Bullish divergence simply means that price is making a lower low while the oscillator makes a higher low. At this point you would consider entering a long position. The next page shows bearish divergence.

Bearish Divergence

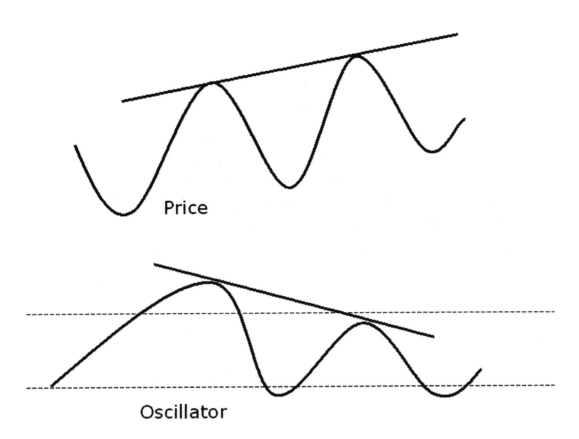

The graph above is showing bearish divergence, and I added trend lines for clearer identification. Bearish divergence simply means that the price is making a higher high while the oscillator makes a lower high. At this point you would consider entering a short position.

Fibonacci Support

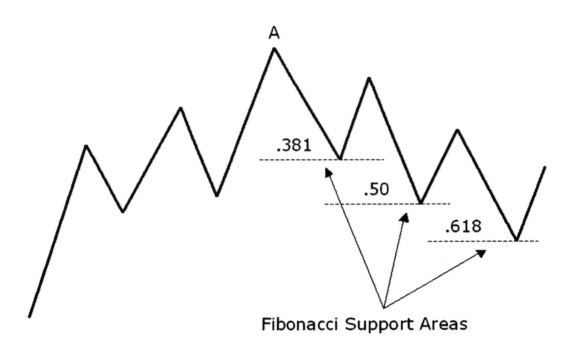

Fibonacci Support Areas

This is a graph showing how Fibonacci numbers can be used for support; however, you should keep in mind that the market is not as perfect as the above chart. A trader should only apply Fibonacci analysis after sufficient training and a thorough understanding of how it should be used with an overall trading plan.

Fibonacci Resistance

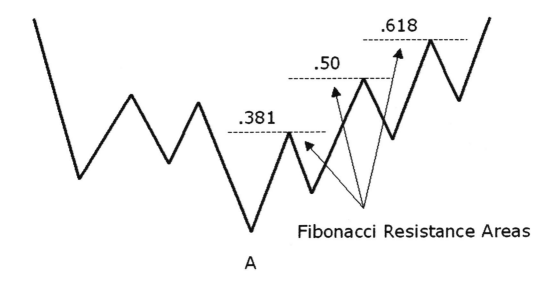

The above graph is showing resistance at commonly used Fibonacci retracements.

CHAPTER 5

Cycles
◻◻◻

Cycles and Swing Points

*T*here are many different terms used in trading, and as mentioned previously, one example is the numerous terms used for turn points. Turn points can also be referred to as peaks and valleys, cycles, cycle points, wave points, and …the list continues.

Every time chart has a dominant trading cycle of between 14 and 25 bars. Most cycles average between 15 and 22 bars from low to low. This sequence can be used to identify the timing of the next turn point beforehand. This approach works considerably well in long time frames such as weekly or monthly charts; however, it can be used on shorter time frames as well.

All price activity is comprised of "swings" of various degrees— minor, intermediate, and major. Every trading cycle bottom is a swing low, and every trading cycle top is a swing high. But, every

---

swing low is *not* a tradable cycle bottom, *nor* is every swing high a tradable cycle top. Between tradable cycle tops and bottoms, there can be one or more swings that are either against the trend or too small to trade.

Methods for identifying Swings and Turn Points

The first method used to identify a swing high or swing low is based on a bar count. For example: A swing high with a strength of five would be defined as a bar with a high that is higher than the high of the five bars preceding it and higher than the high of the five bars following it. This method does not ensure that a swing high of five will be followed by a swing low of five—several swing highs or lows of different strengths may be encountered before a swing low of five occurs. This technique is useful in drawing trend lines.

The second method is to define a reversal in price movement based on a percentage of price movement or number of points. Before the turn point can be confirmed, the reversal must occur after a suspected turn point high or low. This method assures that a turn point high will always follow a turn point low, and that a turn point low will always be followed by a turn point high. This technique is very effective in most dynamic cycle analysis studies.

The third method is to use an oscillator to determine where cycles occur. There are many different ways to accomplish this. I will review two of them. The first way would be to identify some type of crossover of the oscillator (whether it is a crossover of itself or some type of moving average crossing over it). The other way to determine where a cycle occurs is to simply identify when the oscillator gets in the overbought or oversold position.

I prefer to use swing points for drawing trend lines. For identifying turn points, I prefer to use the second method outlined on the previous page (based on reversal in price movement). Following are a few examples of swings.

Swing High

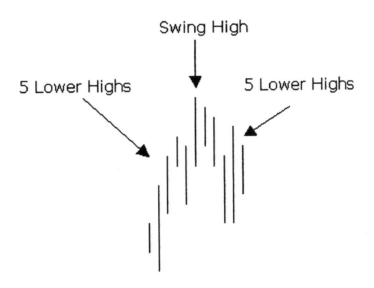

Above is an example of a swing high of 5. A swing high of 7 would have 7 lower highs on each side.

Swing Low

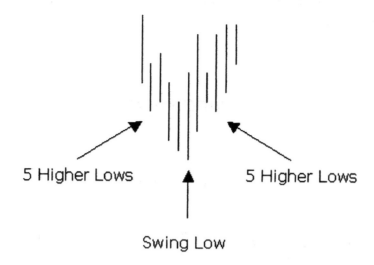

5 Higher Lows   5 Higher Lows

Swing Low

This graph shows a swing low of 5. A swing low of 3 would have 3 higher lows on each side.

The graph on the next page will show swing points with a strength of three.

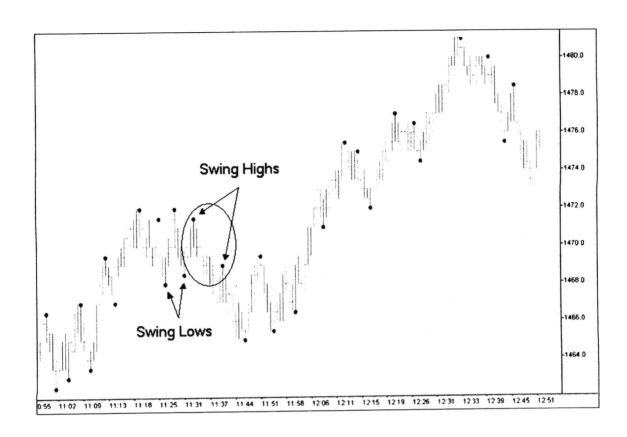

This chart shows swing highs and swing lows. All the dots at the bottom of the prices are swing lows, and all the dots at the top of the prices are swing highs. In this chart there are five swing highs without a swing low in between. Notice the two consecutive swing highs in the oval. This is why I prefer the second method reviewed previously for calculating turn points (which identifies a reversal in price movement based on a percentage or a number of points). The next chart displays swing highs, swing lows, and turn point highs and lows.

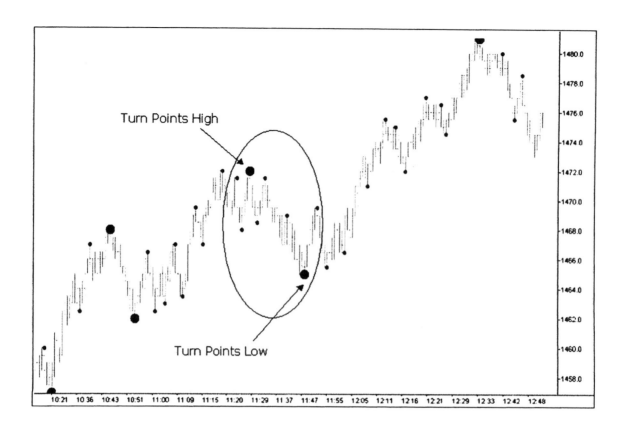

The larger dots at the top and bottom of the prices are turn points; the small dots are swing points. Under most of the larger dots are also swing points as seen on the previous page. Notice the difference where there is a turn point high, followed by a turn point low and this pattern will continue. This method of calculating turn points ensures never having two turn point highs, or two turn point lows in a row, as you can have using swing highs and lows.

CHAPTER 6

Waves of the Market

Identifying Different Waves

One of the greatest American rock 'n' roll bands (The Beach Boys) recorded and released a song called *Catch A Wave* (written by Brian Wilson and Mike Love, both members of The Beach Boys), and the song goes in part like this: "Catch a wave and you're sitting on top of the world." When a surfer paddles out into the ocean, they usually sit on their surfboard waiting for the ideal (big enough) wave to ride. If they tried to catch every wave that came along they would exhaust themselves, and some waves wouldn't carry them very far. That is why they patiently wait for the one that is large enough—the one that makes it all worthwhile.

So it is with a prudent trader—he patiently waits for the right wave or *the right swing in the market price,* to enter the trade. The idea is to come up with a percent of price movement that filters out the unwanted price movements—much like a dedicated surfer waiting for the right wave.

As covered in Chapter 5, there are many different degrees of price swings in the market. Basically there are three that are used most commonly by traders—minor, intermediate, and major. I have found the minor price swings too small to worry about, and almost impossible to trade. Regardless of the degree of the price swing, it is imperative that it has enough movement between the highs and lows to qualify as a tradable swing. Only then would it be identified as a qualified swing (turn point). Otherwise, you will break even at best—or take small losses that will eventually deplete your capital. The main objective is to find swings that have enough movement to generate a profit.

There is a way to measure the amplitude of the move, thereby eliminating the noise (minor price swings). This can be accomplished by creating a filter that will eliminate the swings that are not tradable.

Market price moves up and down in various degrees of swings, or waves within a wave, and so on. This may be confusing to many, but using a filter will enable the trader to measure, number, and classify the waves. Turn points (qualified price swings) are imperative in the use of many theories—The Elliott Wave Theory, Dow Theory, and many other theories, including mine.

The calculation used for the filter to find tradable price swings (turn points) is not complex—it uses the basic math functions of multiplying and dividing. In contrast to many other methods, there is no confusion with measuring the price swing among traders. You could take several people and give them the same chart and the same mathematical procedure, and they would all come back reporting the same results. Filters are covered in Chapter 7.

Therefore, for this method to work the trader would need to find the smallest wave (swing in price) that can be established as a tradable turn point.

The following charts will show different degrees of price swings.

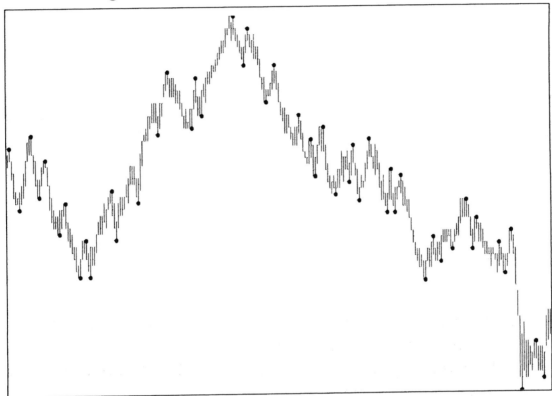

The above chart shows degrees of minor swings (turn points). There is very little price movement between swings (turn point highs and lows). No sooner would you enter a trade, than you would need to exit, or reverse your position.

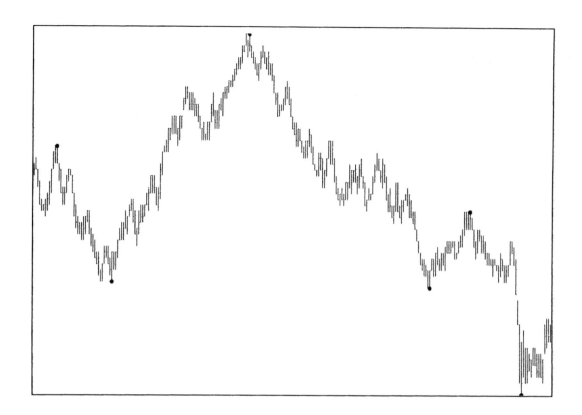

This chart demonstrates intermediate swings (tradable turn points). There is enough price movement between the swings (turn points) for a trader to be reasonably confident that there is sufficient room for profit before the market turns again.

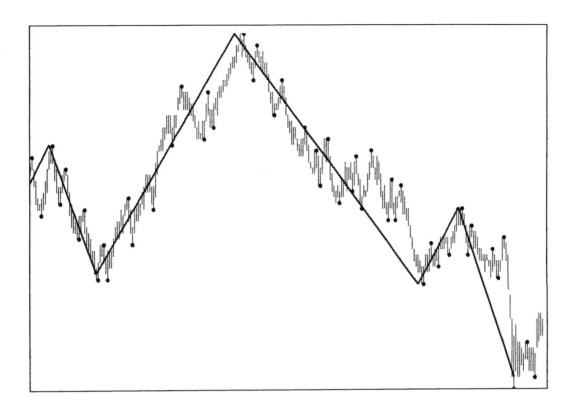

To show the overlay of the minor and intermediate turn points, I connected the intermediate turn points with a line. Notice the price movement between the intermediate turn points. These are the minor swings (turn points), and are not tradable because there is not enough price movement to make a profit.

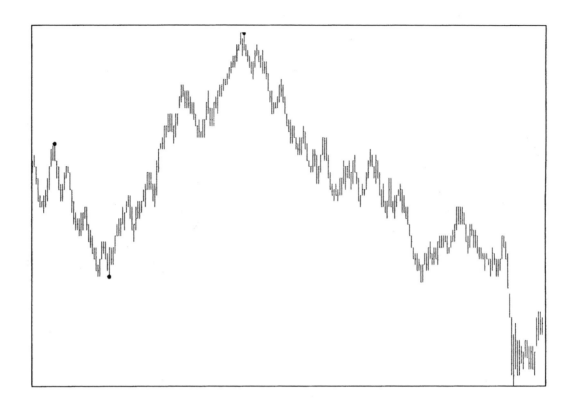

These are the major price swings—note that there are only three plotted on the above chart. On the minor swing chart there were forty-eight swings (turn points). On the intermediate chart there were six. It is the major swings (turn points), and the intermediate ones that I use for trading. The major swings (turn points) show the longer moves; however, the trade is entered on the intermediate swing (turn point).

Each turn point cannot be measured until it is first identified. The challenge with this is that the trader never really knows that there is a turn point until the next one is verified. However, there are ways to increase the odds in your favor which will be covered in more detail later in the book.

CHAPTER 7

Dynamic Waves

···

Identifying Waves

*I*f you are feeling overwhelmed, you can rest a little easier knowing that there are many custom indicators available in the marketplace to eliminate the need for a trader to be a mathematician. I have designed many different indicators that will identify turn points of various degrees, and there is more information in Appendix B on which indicators can be used to show different degrees of price swings. However, to better understand trading, it is important to understand, to some degree, how these indicators work.

The trader needs to establish what the smallest wave they intend to trade will be. On the following pages, I will cover how to identify and measure waves.

Measuring the Waves

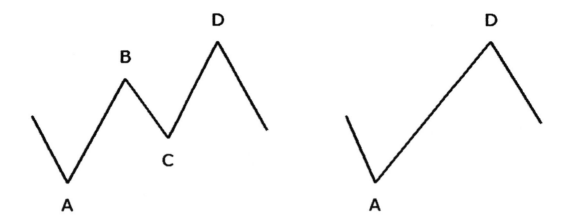

This is how *Trigger-Happy Clyde* would trade the turn points A, B, C, and D on the graph above. He would have bought a little above turn point "A", exiting the trade around turn point "C" from the retracement of turn point "B", thinking the market was going against him. *Clyde* would buy again a little above turn point "C" and exit the trade about the time the market retraced back from turn point "D" to turn point "C". He would break even at best on the first trade, and lose money on the second one. If he had added a filter of 10%, he would have eliminated the losses.

On the other hand, *Ready Freddy* already knew he needed to identify the trend ahead of time; therefore, he started to use filters a long time ago. He knew that the market, on an average, usually moves about 10% between waves (turn points). *Freddy* knew that the market had to move 2% or greater to meet the criteria as a tradable wave (turn point). By using a 2% filter for the entry from turn point "C", he would have been in a good position for profit (or a small loss if the market had whipsawed and gone against him). However, knowing that a 2% filter is needed before the market usually moves to the 10% filter mark, he is in much better shape for making a profit than most traders. If the trade goes in his favor, he knows the profit target will be around the top of the 10% mark at turn point "D".

The graph below shows the turn point measured in percentages.

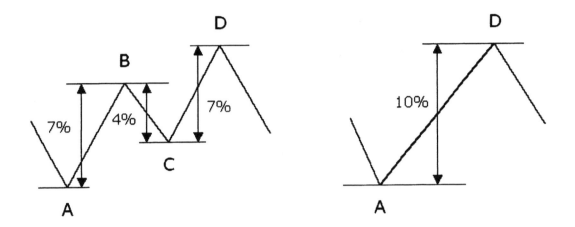

To measure the wave movement between turn point "A" and turn point "B", subtract turn point "A" from turn point "B" and divide it by turn point "A". That will give us the percentage of the move. The math would look like this: Round [(B-A)/A]. By evaluating each tradable turn point, we can find the size of the filter needed to eliminate the noise, and find the tradable turn points.

Reversal Signal

The graph below shows an example of using a 2% filter. *As the price has been decreasing,* newer lows are occurring. At each new low, we would multiply the low price by 102% to get our reversal signal.

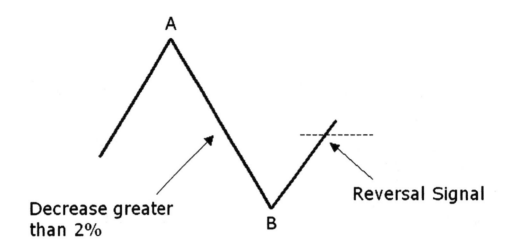

Now we can be reasonably sure that the market will continue in an upward move. We base our assumption on our filter because we have back tested it and have found the percent to eliminate the untradeable turn points.

To better understand the mathematics behind this, let's take a closer look. On the above graph we will put a price of 257 for turn point "A", and at turn point "B" we will put a price of 234. To get the degree of the move, we subtract turn point "B" from turn point "A", then we divide that amount by turn point "A" and that gives us the percent of the move (0.0894941). We then round it and get 9%, and that's the percentage of the move. Therefore, the result of the equation: Rounded (257-234)/257 is 9%. If we want to use this as a filter, we would need to wait for the price to move 9% before identifying it as a valid swing in the market.

Knowing the move from turn point "A" to turn point "B" was 9% or greater, we next want to confirm turn point "B" by looking for a 2% move from the turn point "B" price. Next we take the price at turn point "B" and increase it by 2% to get our reversal signal. The math would look like this: (234*2%) + 234 = 238.68, *or 234*102%=238.68.*

We would confirm a reversal signal when the market reaches a price of 238.68. If the market does not trade in the exact values generated we would need to round our price to the closest market price. For an example, we know that the S&P 500 moves in 0.10 increments; therefore, we would round the price to 238.70. It is better to round up from a low pivot and better to round down from a high pivot.

As the price is now increasing, higher highs are occurring, therefore we would keep track of each new high and would multiply the high price by 98% to get our reversal signal. Our filter of 2% would be the confirmation needed for turn point "B". For an example we will use a high price of 239.00. The math would look like this: 239-(239.00*2%) = 234.22 *or 239*98%=234.22.* The graph shown on the following page illustrates this.

The percent needed for the filter is calculated based on the price movement of the market being traded. For that reason, the trader needs to find the tradable turn points for that particular market, and then calculate the needed percentage for the filter.

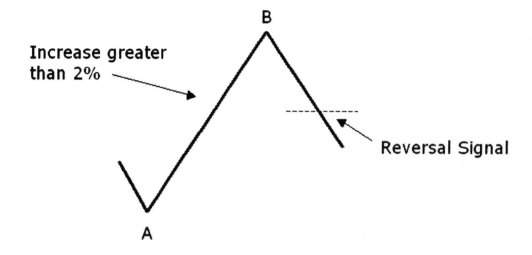

Nothing is done until the price declines to the reversal signal using the 2% filter. After this occurs we have a qualified turn point at "B". At this point we can plot the turn point on the chart as a qualified turn point.

Side by Side Illustration

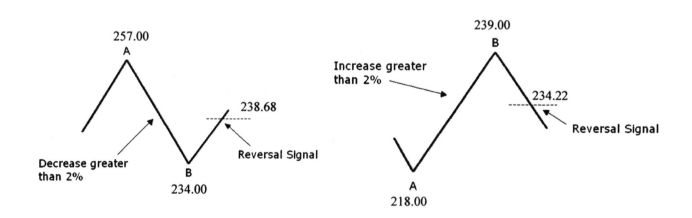

Reversal from a low
using a 2% filter

Reversal from a high
using a 2% filter

Completing The Wave

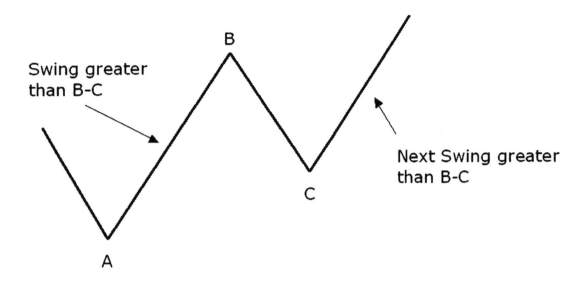

Swing greater than B-C

B

C

A

Next Swing greater than B-C

For a complete swing to qualify, the swing from turn point "B" to turn point "C" must be less in value than the swing from turn point "A" to turn point "B", and the swing from turn point "C" up must be greater than the previous swing from turn point "B" to turn point "C". That's the completed pattern.

The following page shows a bearish down pattern.

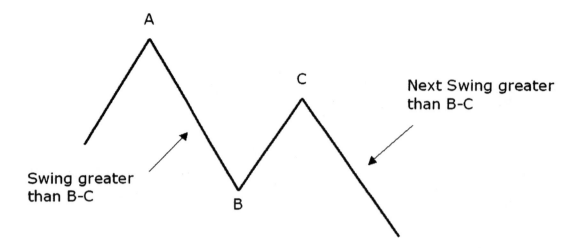

A bearish swing would have the swing between turn point "A" and turn point "B" greater than the swing from turn point "B" to turn point "C", and the swing from turn point "C" down must exceed the previous swing. This is the completion of the pattern.

CHAPTER 8

Advanced Long Entry

The Principle

*T*here are countless chart patterns and each person will have an opinion as to which one(s) are the most effective. However, from my years of experience, I feel that the one shown in this chapter to be the most consistent for identifying and executing a trade. Trading is not always easy and there are many different, and sometimes difficult, decisions that must be made in determining which chart patterns and rules you will use in your trading.

Because analyzing charts is not a precise science, it calls for independent action on the part of the trader. It is of importance that you, as a trader, understand that there are no absolutes in trading. As distressing as this may be to *Slow Moe*, trading is based on theories and hypotheses, which in turn are based on what works the greater percentage of the time (an analytic's nightmare).

Long Entry

To help understand the chart patterns we will be covering in this chapter, envision walking up a staircase. Each stair you step up on is higher than the one below it. When you are walking down, each step is lower than the one above it. The market moves similarly in nature to a staircase; however, each step is not equal in value. Therefore, it is not easy finding each step in the market because you don't know exactly where it will occur until after it reveals itself. There are common areas where the market usually pivots, and these areas are usually found at floor support and resistance, or Fibonacci retracement areas.

Remaining on the side of caution, a trader may choose to enter a trade on the retracement back to where the first turn point occurred. When this occurs, and the first turn point is not taken out (the price does not move past the first turn point), we establish a trend reversal—often referred to as an A, B, C, or P1, P2, P3. "A" would be the first established turn point. The one the market would retrace from would be "B", and therefore, the trader would be looking for "C" to set up to confirm a reversal in the market. The basic trade setup involves three turn points: A, B, and C. The very basic concept is that turn point "C" needs to be greater than turn point "A". On the next page there is a bar chart that demonstrates this basic pattern.

A favorable place to enter a long trade would be on the retracement from turn point "C" (as long as the price at turn point "C" stays above turn point "A"). This would indicate a possible trend reversal setup (see chart below).

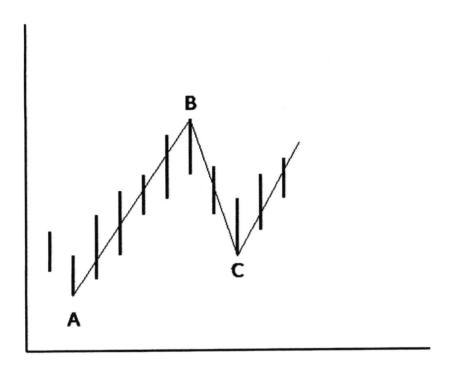

In this chart we use a filter of 3% to establish turn point "A". To identify turn point "B" we used a filter of 1.5% (filters were covered in Chapter 7). To enter the trade we would use the following formula:

Entry Price = C + [(B-A)/4]

Another formula for the entry price would be C+(C*.025). However, there is usually more needed than just the above formulas. It helps to have trend line support at turn point "C" and/or Fibonacci support. The following graph shows a preferential setup.

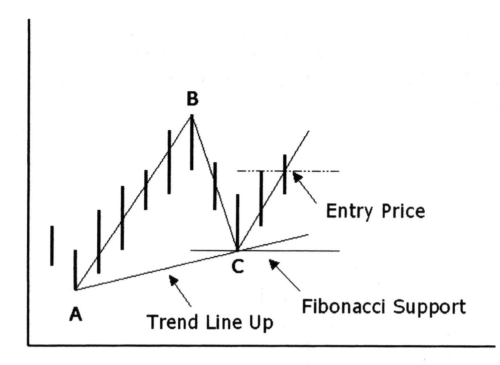

I would consider this to be one of the most promising of setups. *Keep in mind—real trading is not this perfect.* The actual trade unfolded in the following order: We found suspected turn point "A" with a 3.5% filter. From each high after suspected turn point "A", we measured with a 1.5% filter until we found suspected turn point "B". The market retraced to a 0.618 Fibonacci support area (although any Fibonacci support area that works for you would apply). The trend lines were extended from turn point "A" to turn point "C" to help find support. Then we would have entered the trade after the market reversed from turn point "C" times 0.025 added to turn point "C" to meet our qualification for the entry. My preferred entry would be: C + [(B-A)/4], as long as it meets my filter as reviewed earlier.

There are many things that cause price movement, and there is always a reaction to the action swings. Notice the action swing and reaction swing on the graph on the following page.

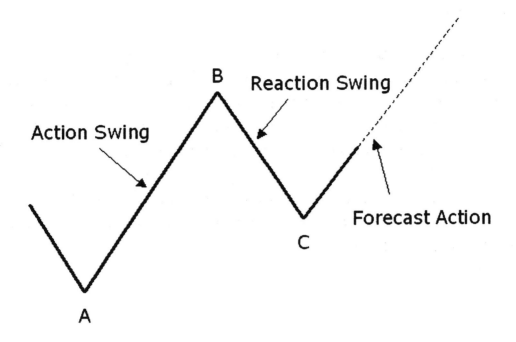

It would be the wisest course to trade the action swings rather than the reaction swings. The main reason for this is that the professional traders, and floor traders, are buying the action swings. They are not trying to trade every swing in the market. That's why we used the setup discussed earlier in this chapter. It is much safer to trade in the direction of the trend.

Critical Price

Since the market can change direction at any turn point, it is reasonable for us to consider the most likely place it may happen. The price where this may occur is at turn point "B", and this price is referred to as the "critical price". Once the market price closes above the critical price, the market will usually continue moving upward toward the profit target. If the price bounces off the critical price, then the market is apt to reverse and start moving down. The more aggressive traders (*Trigger -Happy Clyde*) would reverse and go short on a retest failure of the critical price area.

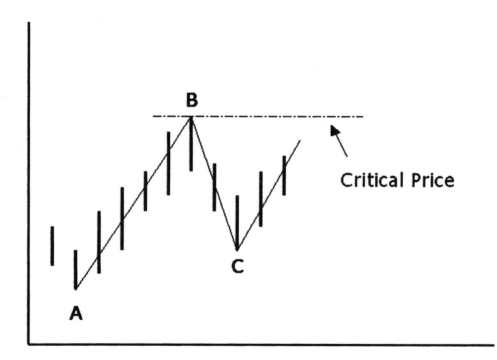

Long Entry Stop

Stops are a very important part of trading. Many traders have lost great sums of money because they did not have a stop in place. You do not want to place the stop too close or you will get stopped out. Neither do you want to place the stop too far away, which would cause you to lose too much money should the trade go against you. Placing a stop somewhere below turn point "C" seems to work well. I like to place it about two ticks (price increments) below turn point "C". Below is a bar chart that shows a fixed stop.

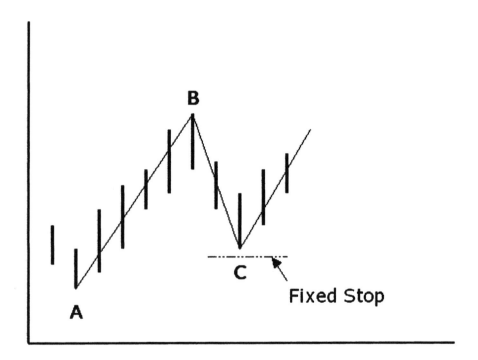

Having a fixed stop in place is a simple process that, if ignored, can cause great havoc. Having a fixed stop in place will ensure reasonably small losses, which in turn, preserves capital—thus the importance!

Long Profit Target

Placing a fixed profit target is more than a good idea. I have seen many traders that have intended to exit a trade at a given profit target, but because they did not have a fixed profit target in place, they were unable to get out of the trade fast enough, and then when the market turned hard against them, it caused them to make small profits at best—or end up with a break-even trade. The market is unmerciful. If it's going in your favor, it seems like forever for it to get to your profit target. However, if it goes against you, it is very fast and furious. Almost all traders will agree that if there is an error made, it will most likely never be in your favor. Placing fixed stops and fixed profit targets can solve unwanted problems. Here's a chart showing the profit target.

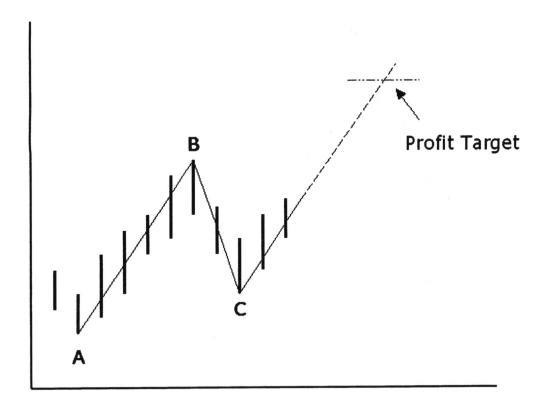

Profit Target = (B – A) + C

It takes about 25% of the move to get into the trade, leaving 75%. I like to leave about 25% for a safety margin to exit the trade. The remaining percentage would be fifty percent for profit.

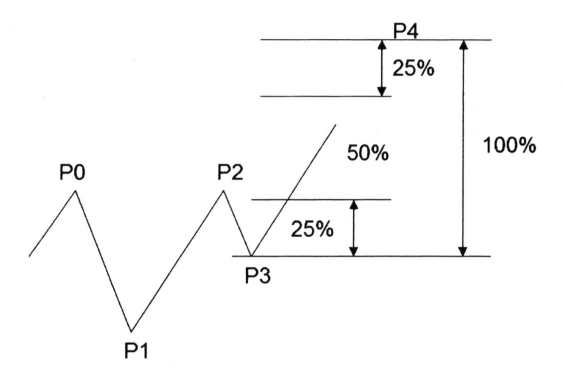

Here's the breakdown: twenty-five percent (25%) to enter, fifty percent (50%) for profit, and twenty-five (25%) to exit.

These are not hard rules—just one way I have found to take profits out of a trade that works well for me. I will later demonstrate other methods to take profits and where to exit trades. Remember—there are different ways of managing money once you are in a trade. You will need to decide the best way that works for you, based on your years of experience, your trading plan, and your capital.

Extended Profit Target

To maximize profits, many investors and traders will trade multiple contracts when trading futures. If you are trading stocks, you can also use this same method. After entering the trade, you would take profit on half of the contracts at your profit target, and then you would move your stop on the remaining ones to break even (your entry price). On the remaining second half, you would take your profit at a Fibonacci extension ratio (1.618 was used in the example below). There are as many different ways to exit a trade as there are traders. I will be covering a few of these techniques for exiting a trade at a profit target; however, each trader will need to decide for himself what works best for him.

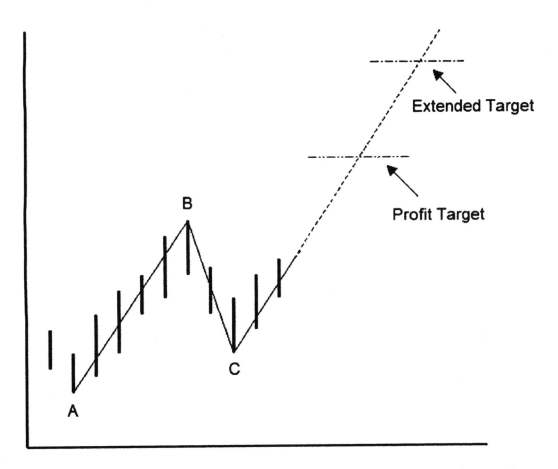

Fibonacci Extended Profit Target = [1.618 (B – A)] + C

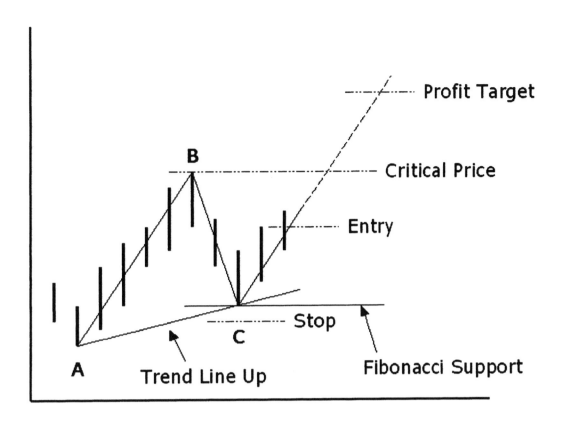

Here is a bar chart that puts it all together with the trend line, Fibonacci support, entry price, stop, critical price, and profit target.

Once the qualification is met to enter a trade, you would want to place your stop, then your profit target. Once the market closes above turn point "B", you can rest a little easier knowing that your trade has a higher probability of being profitable.

If you should get stopped out, the reasonable course would be to re-enter at the next swing low, but only if that swing is above turn point "A". The re-entry technique is reviewed in Chapter 10.

CHAPTER 9

Advanced Short Entry

The Principle

A sell setup (shorting the market) is just the opposite of a long setup (buying the market). There is money to be made on both sides of the market. Once a reversal to the down side is identified, a trader would be in a position to short the market. Some would say that shorting the market is like gambling—that is not true. If a trader has a good understanding of the market, the risk is the same as entering a long position. The market should never be viewed as gambling. There are many who view it as such, but it is not the frame of mind you need to be in to become successful in the market.

Short Trades

To better recognize the chart pattern for shorting the market, imagine walking down a set of stairs. Each step you step down is lower than the one above it. There are common areas where the market usually pivots, and these are usually found at floor support and resistance, or Fibonacci retracement areas.

A good place to enter a short trade would be on the retracement from turn point "C" (as long as the price at turn point "C", stays below turn point "A"). This would indicate a possible trend reversal setup (see chart below).

Turn point "A" would become the first established turn point, then turn point "B" would need to be confirmed as a qualified turn point, followed by turn point "C" setting up for an entry to confirm a reversal in the market.

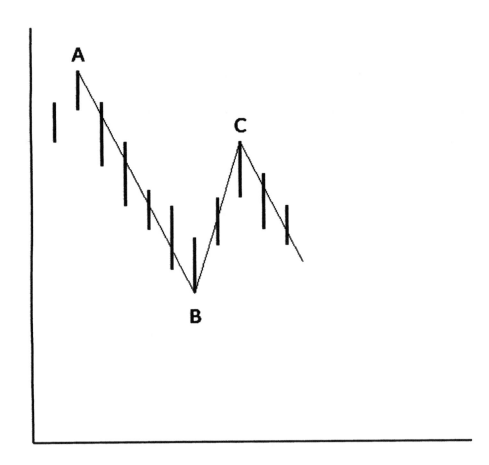

Here we are using a filter of 3.5% to confirm turn point "A". To identify turn point "B", we use a filter of 1.5%. To enter the trade, we would subtract turn point "B" from turn point "A", divide the result by 4, and then subtract that number from turn point "C". Or, we could multiply turn point "C" by 0.025 and subtract the result from turn point "C". It helps to have trend line or Fibonacci resistance at turn point "C".

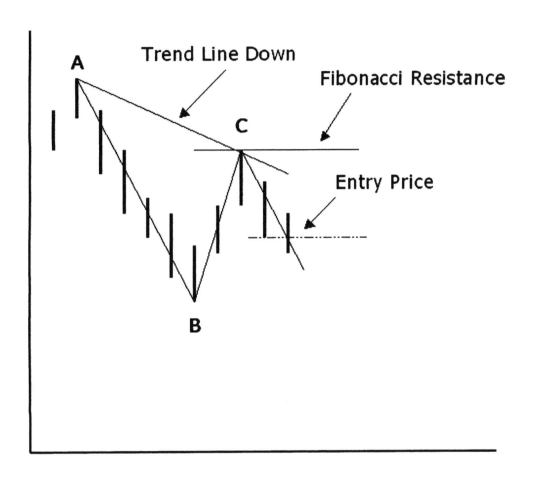

$$\text{Entry Price} = C - [(A - B) \div 4]$$

The above chart shows resistance at turn point "C" and/or Fibonacci resistance.

This would be a nice setup for shorting the market—unfortunately; trading is not always this perfect. Turn point "A" was found using a 3.5% filter. After turn point "B" was confirmed, the market retraced to a 0.618 Fibonacci resistance area (in reality, any Fibonacci support area would apply). The trend lines were extended to help find resistance. The entry was executed after the market reversed from turn point "C" minus the price move to meet the qualification for the entry. One entry would be C-[(A-B)/4], (as long as it meets the calculated filter as reviewed earlier). Another way you could enter the trade would be to multiply the high price at turn point "C" by .025. The formula for the entry price would be C-(C*.025). There is no rule that says .025 is the best value to use, rather it is only a guide. With some experimentation you may prefer to use a different value.

The action and reaction swings for a bearish move would look like this.

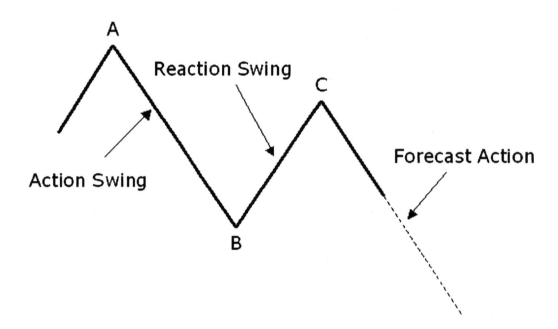

The reaction swings are often shorter in duration. It is always safer to enter a trade in the direction of the trend.

Short Entry Stop

Placing stops is crucial. Stops protect against large losses. In this illustration we will use a stop two ticks (price increments) above turn point "C". The graph below shows a good placement for the stop.

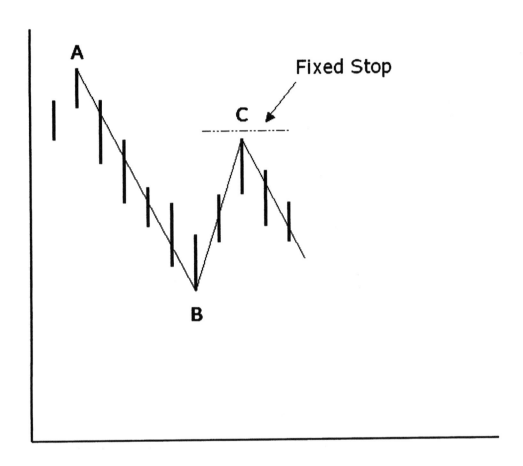

Having a fixed stop in place will assure reasonably small losses, which in turn, helps to maintain capital—a very good thing.

Short Profit Target

Having a fixed profit target is an absolute must! By having your stop(s) and profit target(s) in place, most problems will be eliminated. The illustration below shows a profit target.

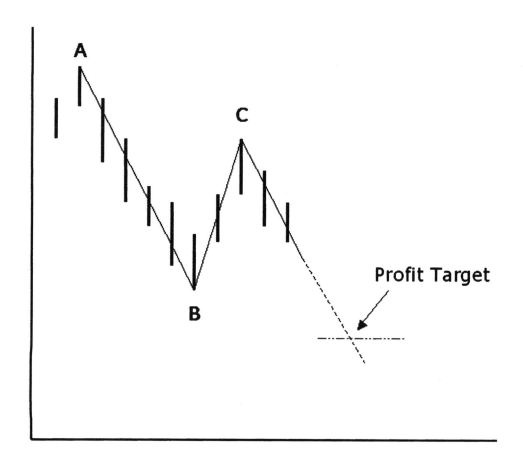

Profit Target = C-(A-B)

Critical Price

After the market price closes below the critical price (a close below turn point "B"), the market will generally move down to the profit target. If the market pivots at the critical price, then the market will usually reverse and start moving up. This does not mean to bail; rather, the best plan is to stick to your trading plan.

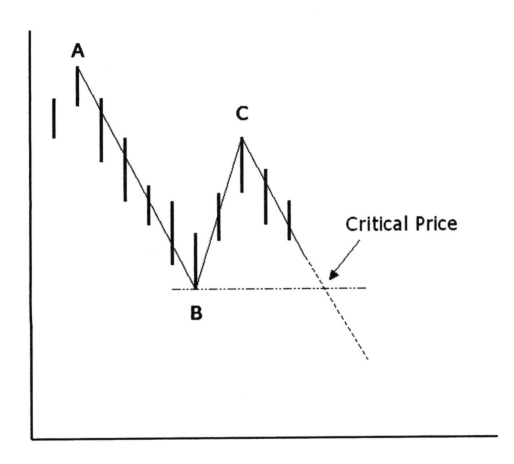

Extended Profit Target

To maximize profits, many investors and traders will trade multiple contracts or shares. After entering the trade, you would take profit on half the number you bought at your profit target and then you would move your stop on the remaining ones to break even (your entry price). On the remaining second half, you would take your profit at a Fibonacci extension ratio (1.618 was used in the example below). There are many variations of exiting out of a trade, and later I will review a few methods.

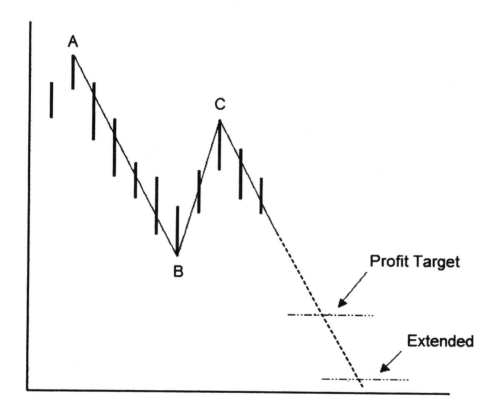

Extended Profit Target = [1.618(A-B)]-C

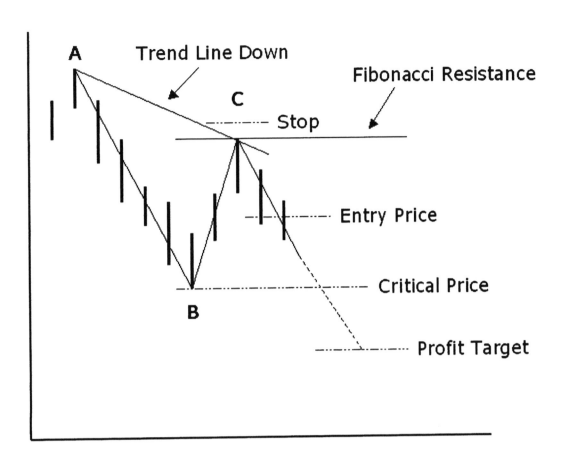

This diagram shows a trend line, Fibonacci resistance, entry price, stop, critical price, and profit target.

After the condition is met and you have entered a trade, you would want to place your stop, and then your profit target. Once the market closes below turn point "B" the trade will, more often than not, go in your favor.

If you should get stopped out, then re-enter the trade on the next swing high, but only if the swing is still below turn point "A". The re-entry technique will be covered in Chapter 10.

CHAPTER 10

Innovative Techniques

Advanced Methods

*T*hese are considered advanced, and progressive methods used in trading. A trader would want to master the information in the earlier chapters before attempting to incorporate these methods into his trading plan.

The Equalization Balance Points analysis technique is a very sophisticated method and requires a great deal of studying and testing to fully understand it. However, the outcome is well worth the endeavor. The Equalization Balance Points is part of my Trident indicator, and gives a trader an edge over other traders. If you elect to use this highly developed method, you need to understand that it takes much research and testing before implementing it.

Scaling out

Here is a diagram showing the targets for scaling out of a trade and how they are laid out. Personally, I do not prefer this method. However, if I were to use this method, Target 1 would have to meet the qualifications discussed in Chapters 8 and 9. I would then calculate Targets 2 and 3 based on Fibonacci ratios.

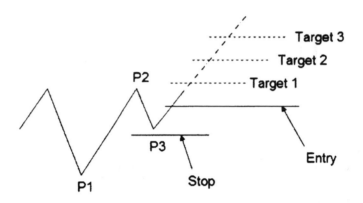

This has become a very popular way of scaling out of trades the last few years. However, most traders do not take into consideration their win/loss and reward/risk ratios. It is imperative that they do. They need to take into account the distance between the profits targets, in relationship to the risk. A common way of trading this method is taking profit of one third of the position size at Target 1 and then moving the stop to breakeven (entry price) plus a tick. Then on the remaining positions there is no real risk.

Before you decide on the best way to take profits, and close out of a trade, be sure you know your win/loss ratio. If there is a time to get somewhat analytic, it would be with the money management part of your trading plan, and this method of exiting a trade further demonstrates this fact.

Adaptive Re-entry Technique

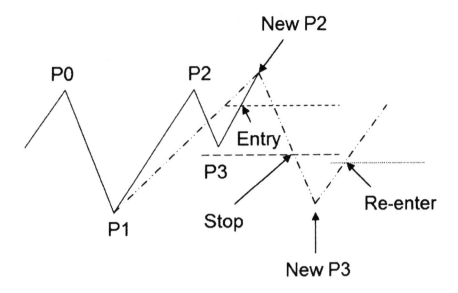

Once a trade is entered on a P3 setup and the market goes against you (stopping you out), it would be prudent to re-enter on the new P3 as shown in the above graph as long as the price does not go below P1.

If you have really deep pockets (millions), it would be reasonable to place your original stop just below P1 for a long entry, and just above P1 for a short entry. However, most traders can't handle that big of a stop even if they do have very deep pockets. The reasonable thing to do, if you are stopped out, would be to re-enter the trade if another setup occurs.

Following the release of the first edition of this publication, it was reviewed by several critics, both in the USA and abroad. One such company that reviews hundreds of trading books was impressed that my book was the only one that they had seen that covered a re-entry technique.

Reversing a Position

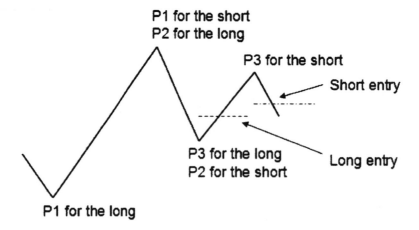

The above graph illustrates the relationship of the turn points and how they change, depending on the direction of the trade setup. As shown on this graph, there was a qualified long setup. Shortly after the long position was entered, the market changed direction and set up a short entry.

Assuming a trader was long, he would have four options:

1. Stay with the long trade until the stop or target was reached.
2. Exit the long on the reversal.
3. Reverse the position.
4. Reverse and double the position size. This means increasing the position size for the short by twice the size of the long position.

A careful study of the above example should be considered in order to determine how you personally will elect to trade this type of setup. This should be done prior to executing the trade. There are no set rules on this—it is solely up to each individual trader. Of the upmost importance is to have a strategy firmly in mind before attempting to add this type of trade to your trading plan.

Position Sizing

Position sizing (sometimes referred to as bet size) is a money management tool. There are many different ways to calculate position sizing. As with other money management decisions, it is up to the individual trader to experiment and decide what works best for him. I would not recommend spending an excessive amount of time on this aspect of your trading, especially if you are still in the development stage of your trading plan. Once you are successfully trading your plan, you may want to implement this type of advanced application.

This is how one trader may determine the amount of contracts he can trade within his trading plan. Here are the variables this trader used in his calculations:

Account Size: 40,000.00

Risk Tolerance: 3% of account per trade = 1,200.00

Stop Loss: | Entry price – Stop | + Cost per trade

Cost Per Trade: 5.00 round trip per contract/per trade.

Margin: Trading the S&P 500 E-mini, the margin for one contract is currently 500.00. He could potentially trade 80 contracts (500.00 x 80) if it did not exceed his risk tolerance.

Our trader is about to enter a trade. His entry for a long is at 1142.50 and his profit target is 1144.50, with a stop placed at 1141.50.

Knowing his entry, his profit target and stop, he knows he can trade (1) contract for a profit of 95.00 (2 points x 50.00-5.00 commissions/fees)—or he could get stopped out for a loss of 55.00 (1 point x 50.00+5.00 commissions/fees). With that information, he calculates how many contracts he can trade without exceeding his risk tolerance level, or exceed his account margin of 80 contracts. Below are his calculations for this particular trade.

Assuming a winning trade: 2 points = 100.00-5.00 = 95.00 potential **Profit** per contract.

or

Assuming a losing trade: 1 point = 50.00+5.00 = 55.00

potential **Loss** per contract.

His Risk Tolerance = 3% of 40,000 = 1,200.00

His risk (stop loss) per point/per contract = 55.00

Position Size = (Risk Tolerance/Risk) = 1200/55 = 21 Contracts

He takes the trade. He goes long with 21 contracts (he does not jump out early or overstay his position). Here are the two possible outcomes:

21 contracts for a 2 point target with a stop loss of 1 point would have resulted in a **Profit** of 1995.00 (21 x 2 = 42 points x 50.00 = 2100.00-105.00 commissions/fees).

or

21 contracts for a 2 point target with a stop loss of 1 point would have resulted in a **Loss** of 1155.00 (21 x 1= 21 points x 50.00 = 1050.00+105.00 commissions/fees).

This is a simplification to show the maximum contracts that this trader could trade (21) and still stay within his rules. Any method that works for you would accomplish the same result. It is just one more way to manage your account and stay within your trading parameters.

Equalization Balance Points

Oftentimes the market will repeat the same cycle over and over again. The formula below is an interesting way of finding where the market will reverse. The algorithms were formulated on the expected balance in the market between buying and selling pressure, which controls the market. The formulas regarding the balance points can invert at times. If this occurs, it usually indicates the market has broken out of congestion, and will correct itself after more price action happens between swings.

Next short-term swing: $B2 = (2*P2)-P0$

Next long-term swing: $B6 = (P2+P\_2)-P\_4$

The B2 and B6 stand for Price Balance Points. The short-term is B2 and the long-term is B6. This is a very complex method of trading. There are varied degrees of swings: minor, intermediate and major. The minor swings are too hard to trade unless you are in the trading pit on the exchange floor. The buy and sell points are the intermediate and major swings. For an explanation of what the different "P" numbers represent, please refer to Chapter 12 (subtitle Reviewing Trend).

Uptrend: If B6 was above B2 for the last swing, and B2 is above B6 for the current swing, **then the P3 turn point should be above B6** and the next **peak** after P3 should terminate an uptrend.

Downtrend: If B2 was above B6 for the last swing, and B6 is above B2 for the current swing, **then the P3 turn point should be below B6** and the next **valley** after P3 will terminate a downtrend.

In both of these rules, the price at P3 is compared against the balance price of B6, which is the long-term balance price. In both of these cases, the P3 will be the last swing in the current trend direction. Beware that a trend reversal is usually imminent.

Terminating an uptrend

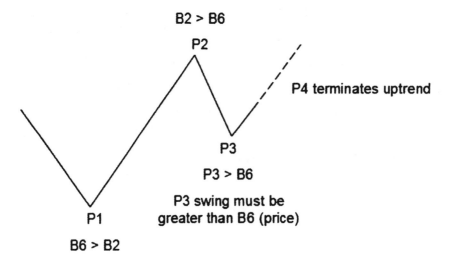

The distance between P3 and P4 can be any length and may not necessarily conform to a potential trade setup to the downside.

Terminating a downtrend

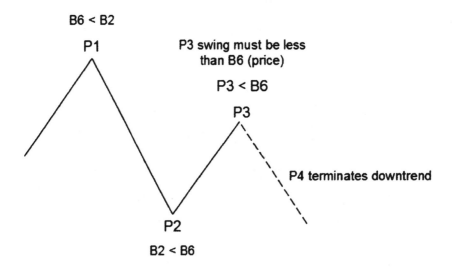

The distance between P3 and P4 can be any length and may not necessarily conform to a potential trade setup to the upside.

CHAPTER 11

Trading Patterns

....

Identifying Tradable Patterns

*T*here are many different chart patterns that are tradable. You will be the only person who can determine which ones you will use in your trading plan. Keep in mind that, from time to time, various trading methods have been mistaken for the Holy Grail, resulting in disturbing amounts of losses when market conditions change. Therefore, the prudent course would be to use a method that works in all markets and in all time frames, and that has withstood the test of time. It is imperative that you, the trader, understand that the larger the time frame of the chart being traded, the more dependable the trading method becomes. Some traders try to trade a one-tick chart, and the consensus of those traders is that the smaller the time frame the better. They will only be butting heads with the floor traders, and they will frequently end up losing money. My research has shown that larger time frames produce a larger amount of favorable trades. By studying a yearly chart, you will observe that trading becomes almost perfect. However, very few traders have the time to wait for profits trading that long of a time frame, and/or will not have the money to trade such a large time frame. As previously discussed in Chapter 1, the rules that a trader chooses to trade by are determined by the amount of money the trader has and his/her mental makeup. Therefore, most traders will trade a daily chart for position trading—long or short-term. And most day traders will trade smaller time frames like a three, five, and twenty minute time chart. As of the writing of this book, I prefer to use tick or volume (share bar) charts.

I feel it is more important to preserve capital than to try and force an opportunity to happen. Opportunity will always be there if you use discernment and good money management skills.

This chapter will provide an overview of what most successful traders consider to be tradable chart patterns. On the intraday graphs shown, a buy indicates a *long* entry, and a sell indicates a *short* entry.

The following chart pattern is the one I consider to be the most effective (as was covered in Chapters 8 and 9).

The diagram on the following page shows the short setup.

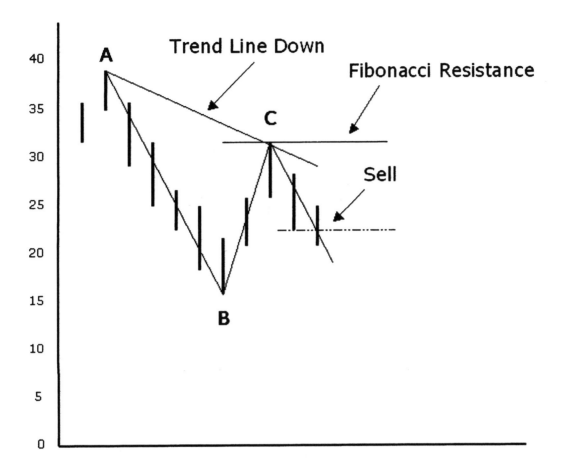

I would sell (short entry) off the retracement from turn point "C" after the trade establishes trend line and Fibonacci resistance. If it meets your qualifications for a short entry, then you would enter the trade.

Dow Pattern

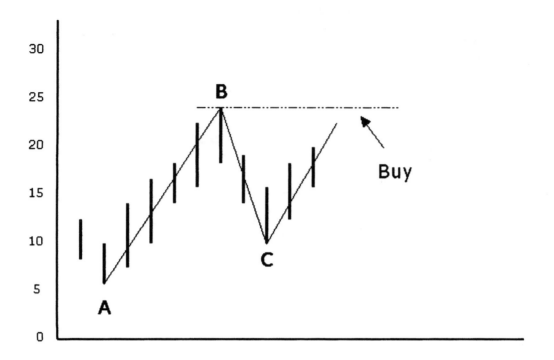

The basic Dow long entry takes place when the price takes out turn point "B". Some traders prefer to see a price bar close above turn point "B" for confirmation. However, in today's markets, the problem with waiting for the price to close above turn point "B" is that it makes the stop very large compared to the profit target.

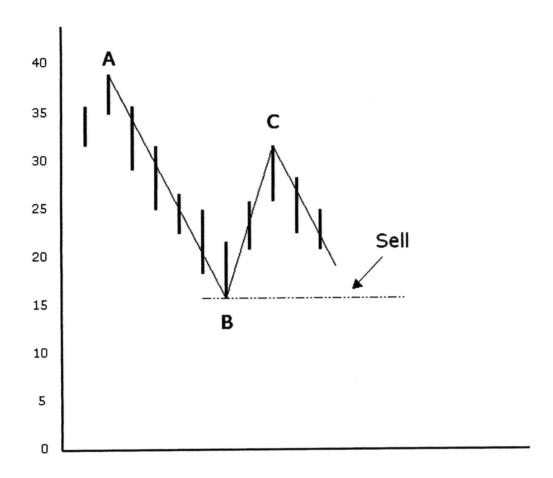

The basic Dow short entry takes place when the price takes out turn point "B". Some traders prefer to see a price bar close below turn point "B" for confirmation.

Divergence

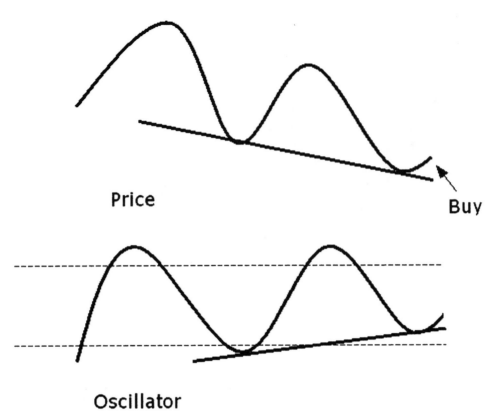

Price

Buy

Oscillator

When bullish divergence occurs (the price moves up and the oscillator turns up), you would enter long (buy). I prefer to measure the move using the filtering technique as outlined in Chapter 7. This helps to establish that the swing is big enough to be tradable.

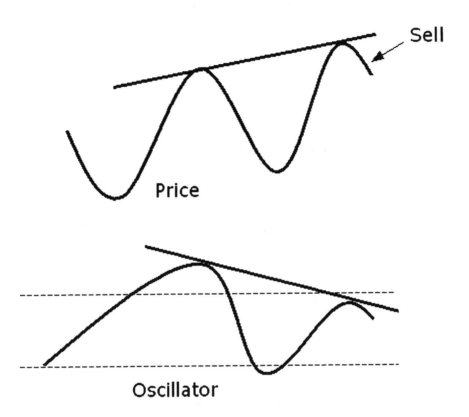

When bearish divergence occurs, (the price moves down and the oscillator turns down), you would enter short (sell). I prefer to measure the move using the filtering technique as outlined in Chapter 7. This helps to establish that the swing is big enough to be tradable.

Head & Shoulders

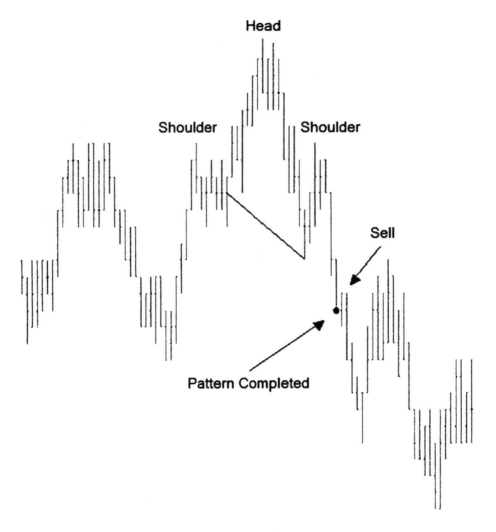

The theory behind the basic Head & Shoulders pattern is that the price has reversed and the market is headed down. Some traders will short at the point where the neckline is broken. Others will short after the pattern is completed.

However, if you look closely at the Head & Shoulders pattern, you will recognize a setup from what we previously learned in Chapter 9. What I have observed about this pattern is that often, right after the pattern is completed, the market usually reverses.

Normal Double Bottom and Double Top Patterns

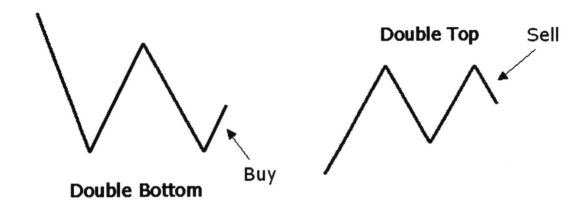

To enter the trade on a double bottom, you would buy after the price retested the low of the previous bottom (last low turn point). For a double top, you would sell after the price retested the previous high (last high turn point).

Trend Line Breaks

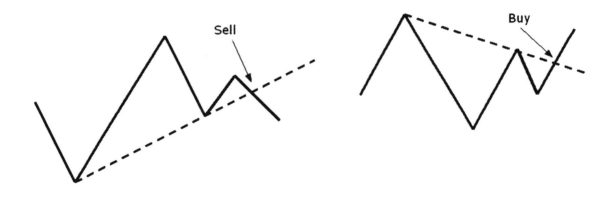

In my opinion, trend line breaks are risky trades, as often times they will whipsaw (reverse in the other direction). The theory is to sell when the price breaks the uptrend line, and to buy when the price breaks the downtrend line.

Triangle breakout failure

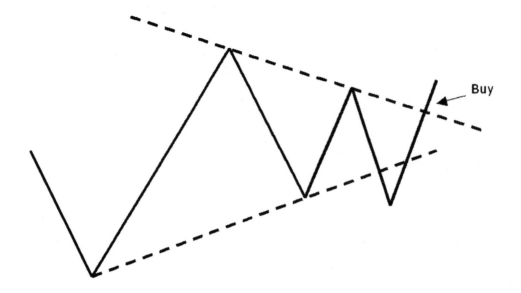

The triangle breakout failure occurs when the price breaks the uptrend line, and then rallies back and breaks above the downtrend line—and that is where some traders would enter a long position.

Triangle breakout failure

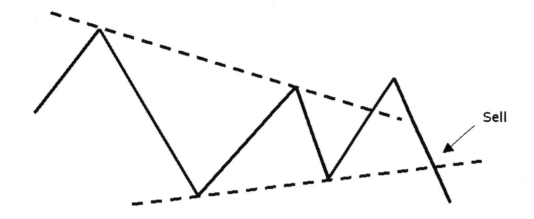

Triangle breakout failure occurs when the price breaks the downtrend line, and then reverses and sells off breaking the uptrend line—and that is where the entry for a short position would be.

Floor Support & Resistance

Many traders rely on floor support and resistance areas to execute a trade, depending on what the price action does once it reaches a support or resistance area. There are many different ways traders calculate these price points; however, the most common way is as follows.

The calculations for these lines are:

Pivot = (High + Low + Close)/3

Support 1 = Pivot * 2 - High
Resistance 1 = Pivot *2 - Low

Support 2 = Pivot - Resistance 1 + Support 1
Resistance 2 = Pivot + Resistance 1 - Support 1

Support 3 = Pivot - Resistance 2 + Support 1
Resistance 3 = Pivot + Resistance 2 - Support 1

Support 4 = Pivot - Resistance 2 + Support 2
Resistance 4 = Pivot + Resistance 2 - Support 2

In Chapters 14 & 15 (which covers trading charts) I will review in more detail how to use support and resistance when trading.

The trading patterns reviewed in this chapter can be enhanced by using the filtering method discussed in Chapters 8 and 9, thus increasing your odds.

CHAPTER 12

Identifying Trend

∙∙

Identification of Trend

The trend may be the hardest thing to explain and identify. You have heard many say to "trade in the direction of the trend", but you might ask, "Which direction are they referring to?" "Which trend are they referring to—long-term, intermediate term, or short-term?" An example: The trend on a weekly chart is up—does that mean that if you were trading a five minute chart you would only be looking to buy every bottom that comes along? If so, you would most likely lose a lot of money. The reason for this is that a weekly chart can be trending up and at the same time the market could move down substantially in one day. One solution to this problem would be to look at a chart three times larger than the one being traded to establish trend direction. For instance, if trading a five minute chart look for the direction of a fifteen minute chart, and if trading a daily chart look for the direction of a weekly chart. It is prudent to trade the intermediate trend.

Establishing Trend

Trend can be identified in many different ways. A few of the most commonly used indicators to define trend are: trend lines, moving averages, trading bands, and trend channels. Following is an example of a trend line and a moving average showing trend direction.

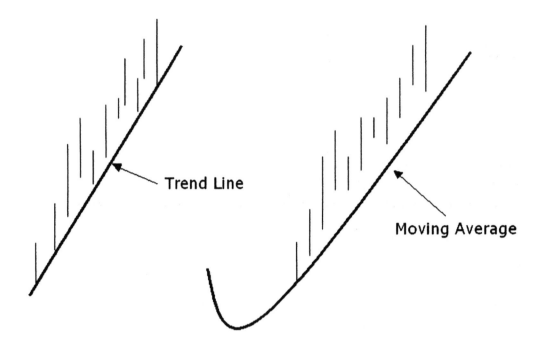

In the above illustration, the market tends to bounce off and stay above the trend line and the moving average, showing that the trend is up. On the next page is a chart showing a trend line on an intraday chart.

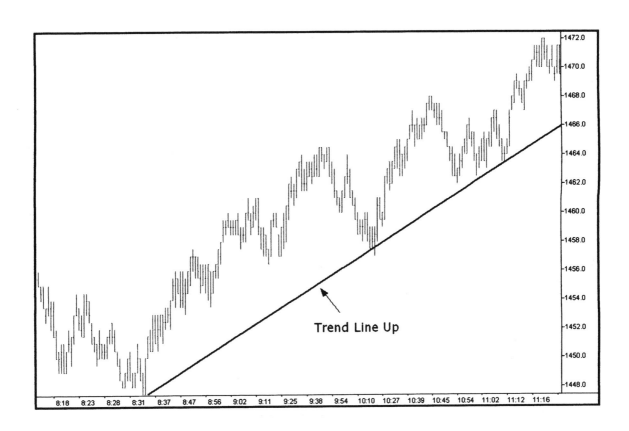

Trend Line Up

The trend line was extended, and the market retraced and found support on it. I prefer trend lines to moving averages. Moving averages are usually good for showing shorter term trends. Trend lines will help show longer term trends.

Many traders use moving averages to help them identify the trend. The following page shows how a moving average can be used to show the overall direction of the trend.

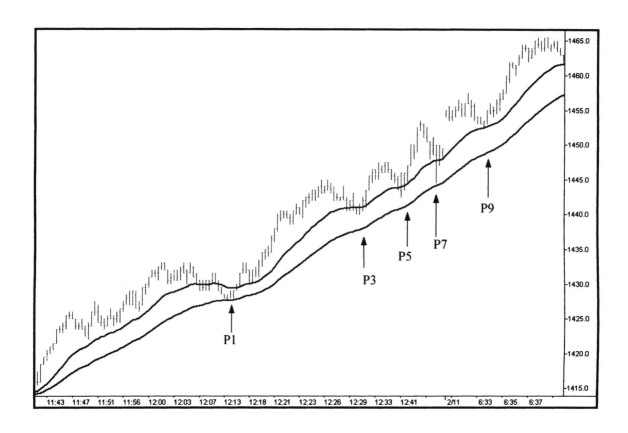

I plotted two EMAs (exponential moving averages) on the above chart. The one on top is a twenty-three length EMA, and the other is a fifty length EMA. Typically, price will turn when it touches, or penetrates, the EMA. On the chart above, the market is trending up, so you would be looking for turn point lows at a support area close to the EMA.

Each turn point low is greater (higher in price) than the previous turn point low, indicating an uptrend. P3 is greater in value than P1, and P5 is greater in value than P3. Until that pattern reverses, the trend should continue up.

Reviewing Trend Reversals

A trend reversal usually occurs in areas with some type of support and resistance. Fibonacci and/or floor support and resistance areas are the ones most generally used. There are many other ways of finding support and resistance areas. You can do this by using Gann lines, Gann fans, Andrew's Pitchfork, Andrew's expanded pivot lines, and astrological (planetary and lunar) lines. I normally use Fibonacci or floor support and resistance areas because they are the easiest to use. The others are more in-depth and require a study all on their own. Price will tend to bounce off an area of support and resistance; however, that in itself is not a very safe place to enter a trade. The below illustration demonstrates the earliest a trader would be reasonably confident that a market reversal is occurring to the upside (bullish reversal pattern).

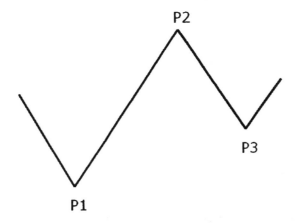

The calculation for a market reversal is that P3 is greater than P1. It is important to remember that nothing is one hundred percent certain. What the trader should be looking for is something that works the majority of the time. The next graph shows a reversal to the downside (bearish reversal).

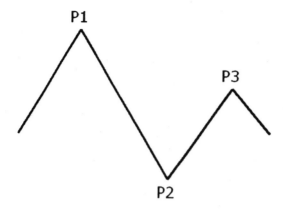

The above illustration demonstrates the earliest a trader would be reasonably confident that a market reversal is occurring to the downside (bearish reversal pattern). The formula for reversal toward the downside is that P3 is less in value than P1.

Key Points about Trend Reversals

If the price moves past P1 and closes above P1, then some of the more experienced traders would then consider entering a trade, or reversing their position. A careful study of this is needed before you would consider adding this type of trade to your trading plan.

Something else to keep in mind is that when a trend reversal occurs, it is at the end of a current trend; therefore, caution is needed. When the market has moved out of the normal range, without a retracement of any real significance, expect some brief consolidation before a reversal occurs. On a really strong trendy day, where the market has moved a considerable amount in price, it would be wise not to consider a trend reversal trade. For an example: Over the last few months the market you were trading was moving an average of fifty points a day, and then it moves out of that range significantly. It would be better to avoid taking any reversal trades; rather, wait for a setup to occur in the direction of the major move.

Reviewing Trend

As reviewed in previous chapters, markets tend to move in channels, and it is important to understand market movement. An uptrending market shows "right translation" in which the market leans to the right as it rises for more price bars than are declining. So the swing (move) from P1 to P2 should be greater than the swing (move) from P2 to P3. From that point forward, each swing up would be greater than the swing down. Right translation would look like the chart below.

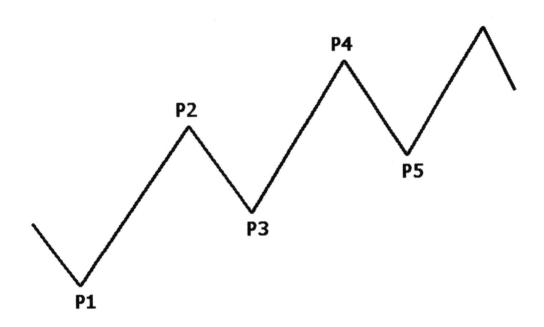

On the above graph, the market has "right translation" and is in an uptrend. P3 is greater than P1, and then P5 is greater than P3, and as long as this pattern continues, the market should keep going up until a trend reversal occurs.

To continue on the subject of market movement, a downtrending market shows "left translation" in which the market leans to the left as it declines for more price bars than are rising. Thus, the swing (move) from P1 to P2 should be greater than the swing (move) from P2 to P3. From that point forward, each swing down would be greater than the swing up. "Left translation" would look like the chart below.

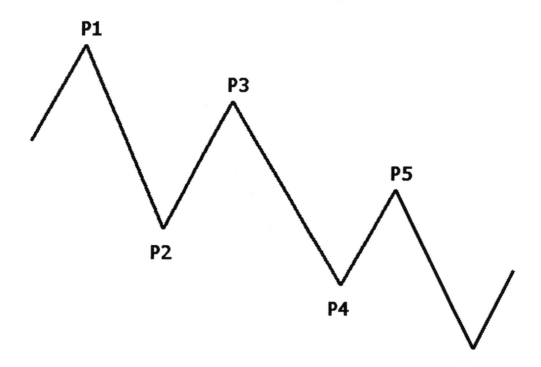

On the above graph, the market has "left translation" and is in a downtrend. P3 is less than P1, and then P5 is less than P3, and as long as this pattern continues, the market should keep going down until a trend reversal occurs.

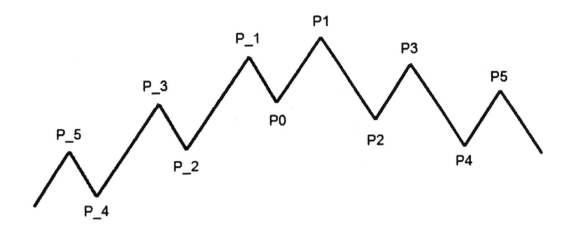

The P1 on this chart would be the highest high turn point. P1 is where the numbering starts from, and as the price moves forward, the next turn point low would be P2, the next turn point high would be P3, and the count would continue. The low turn point before P1 would be P0, the previous turn point high would be P_1, and the count would continue backward. The series of numbers going forward can be endless until a new low P1 is formed, meaning P1 would need to be confirmed by a reversal to the upside.

The series of numbers appearing on the graph are: P_5, P_4, P_3, P_2, P_1, P0, P1, (P1 starts the count), P2, P3, P4, and P5.

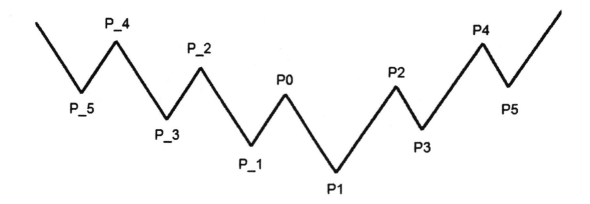

The P numbers are a way to identify and label various turn points. As pointed out in previous chapters, everyone labels turn points differently. P1 is where I like to start my count from, whether it is a highest high or lowest low turn point. The chart above shows P1 as the lowest low.

P1 is where the numbering starts from, and as the price moves forward, the next turn point high would be P2, the next turn point low would be P3, and the count would continue. The high turn point before P1 would be P0, the previous turn point low would be P_1, and would continue backward. The series of numbers forward can be endless until a new P1 high is formed, meaning P1 would need to be confirmed by a reversal to the downside.

The series of numbers appearing on the graph are: P_5, P_4, P_3, P_2, P_1, P0, P1, (P1 starts the count), P2, P3, P4, P5.

Trend Trades

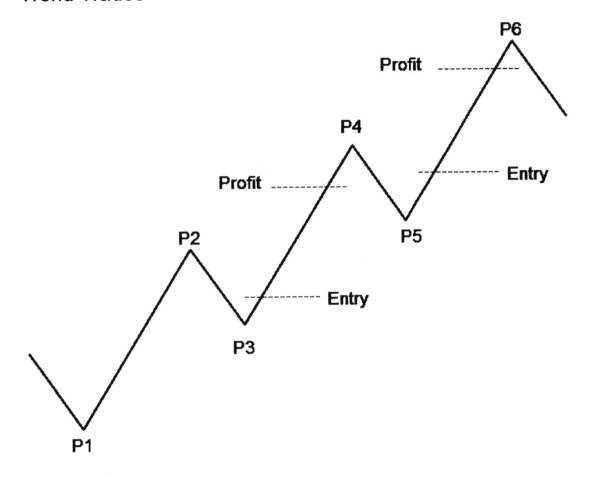

In this graph, the trend reversal occurred and the trade would have been entered just above P3, then the market moved up to reach the target. As long as P4 is greater in value than P2, and P5 is greater in value than P3, and assuming that the rest of the trade setup meets our rules (trading plan), a long trade would be placed just above the turn point at P5. This type of trend trading could continue until a trend reversal happens. It's noteworthy to keep in mind that as of the writing of this book, most day traders feel the market moves in waves of three; meaning, most feel the market will reverse on the third wave. I recommend that before implementing any new methods or theories (such as this one) into your trading plan, you conduct a real-time study beforehand.

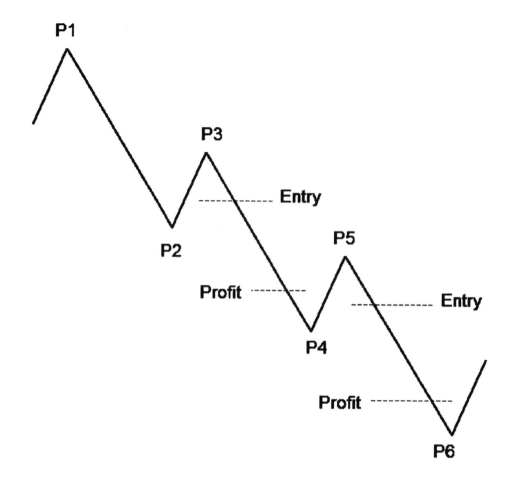

In this graph, the trend reversal occurred and the trade would have been entered just below P3, then the market moved down to reach the target. As long as P4 is less in value than P2, and P5 is less in value than P3, and assuming that the rest of the trade setup meets our rules (trading plan), then a short trade would be placed just below turn point P5. This type of trend trading could continue until a trend reversal happens.

CHAPTER 13

Time Tested Methods

Trading Patterns That Have Endured

Over the years there have only been a few trading methods that have been able to withstand the test of time. Since the beginning of the stock market, we have seen a few stock market crashes. Some not as bad as others, and in the last few decades the market has recovered rather quickly. One of the worst stock market crashes of all time was in 1929 – 1933. The market fell 71.2% in a few months, and took years to recover. Had someone been using my method and theories, they would have been in a cash position and no harm would have come to them in regards to their investment in the market.

Some say, "Wait for the news, and then trade the news." I strongly believe that if you wait on the news to trade, you won't last long in the trading world. I have found it to be true that the news is already built into the charts before it happens. This will be evident as you look at the charts in this chapter.

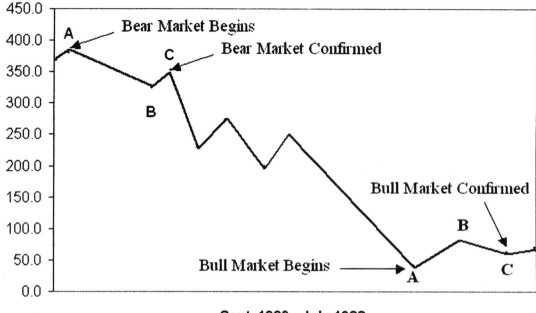

INDU

Sept. 1929 - July 1933

As you can see in the above diagram, the A, B, C pattern would have pinpointed the sell-off far in advance of the market dropping off 71.2%.

An interesting bit of information is that during the days of the great stock market crash, hundreds of investors were *not* jumping out of windows, and there were *no* suicides committed. Rumors circulate, which later become stories, and then develop into what is relayed as factual, and this was just one of those situations.

The chart on the following page reviews a chart from 1987, showing how an investor could have predicted the market's sell-off before losing a great deal of money.

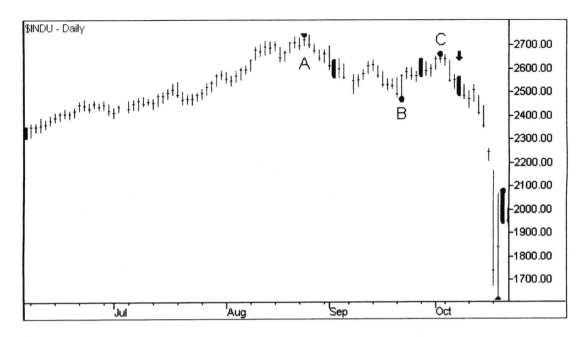

This chart is a Dow Jones Industrial of 1987. From August 25, 1987 to October 20, 1987 the market dropped 1,130.50 points in a little less than two month's time. This sell-off caught many investors by surprise and many lost a great deal of money exiting their long positions as fast as they could, thinking the market would keep selling off.

The market went from a high of 2746.70 to a low of 1616.20. To illustrate my point on how easily the sell-off could have been identified, I plotted a single indicator of mine (Turn Points) on the above chart. Based on what was covered in Chapter 9, we can easily see the A, B, C pattern setting up. If an investor had been holding long positions at that time, it would have been clear to go to a cash position (or start looking for an opportunity to short the market). Turn point "A" occurred on August 25, 1987 with a high price of 2746.70, turn point "B" occurred on September 22, 1987 with a low price of 2468.99, resulting in a drop of 277.71 points. At that time it was not uncommon for the market to move 50+ points a day. Turn point "C" was confirmed on October 2, 1987. What happened next was a phenomenal drop to 1616.20 by October 20, 1987, a total move of 1130.50 points.

A more recent example of traders and investors being caught off guard (and losing a great deal of money) as the market plummeted is the bear market that started January 14, 2000 with the Dow at 11749.97.

Savvy investors were already in cash, or shorting (selling) the market. Because they knew the real downtrend started on January 14, 2000, these investors should have been shorting the market from that point forward. The market came close to testing the high of April 12, 2000, but never went higher. The following chart demonstrates the point where the downtrend was confirmed. The most interesting point is that about two years after the fact, the news media starting reporting that we were in a bear market. Isn't that amazing? Just about the time they reported we were in a bear market, the market turned up and started to reverse to the long side (bullish).

The above chart clearly shows the reversal to the downside (bearish). The market put in a high on January 14, 2000 and a downtrend was confirmed on April 14, 2000.

If a trader missed the first setup showing a bear market, there were a few more warnings after this. The market tried testing the high of January 14, 2000 on April 12, 2000, September 6, 2000, and May 22, 2001. On May 22, 2001, there was another A, B, C to the downside. Anyone using the method in Chapter 9 had not one, but three different warnings to recognize and identify a bear market.

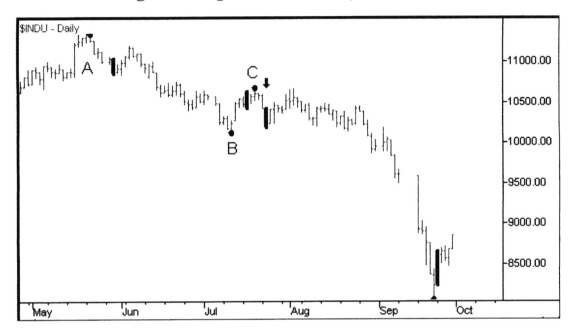

This chart clearly shows the setup for the last leg down in the sell-off. The A, B, C started on May 22, 2001, followed by turn point "B" on July 11, 2001. Turn point "C" formed on July 19, 2001, and was confirmed on July 24, 2001. There was enough time for most traders to get in a cash position, or a short position, before the low of 8062.34 occurred that rattled everyone's nerves on September 20, 2001, with a percentage loss of 31.38% from the high of January 14, 2000. The price rallied from September 20, 2001, but later sold off again down to a new low of 7197.00 on October 10, 2002, with a percentage loss of 38.74% from the high of the Dow.

Obviously those who had a working knowledge of the market, good money management skills, and a trading method that worked, were able to avoid the pain and agony that comes with losing money in the markets. In the previous examples, traders who had a reliable trading method would not have lost money in the market because they would have been in cash, or in short positions.

CHAPTER 14

Viewing Trading Patterns

....

Reviewing Chart Patterns and Setups

*I*n the following chapters I will cover information on how various indicators are used in establishing trade setups. Most of the custom indicators can be substituted with standard indicators; however, as a rule, custom indicators perform better. I showed trades that were taken, along with some trades that I missed, over a period of a few months. I tried to include a variety of trades (some good, some not so good) in order to facilitate the recognition of several different trade setups.

The dictionary is the only place where "success" comes before "work". Becoming a successful trader isn't easy—if it were, then everyone would be doing it. Most of those who do achieve profitability will tell you that they owe their success to hard work and study. There are numerous stories where traders put in a heroic effort and are rewarded with huge profits, but they have difficulty keeping up the pace. Over time they burn out. They use up all their energy

---

and end up leaving the profession. Anyone can make it as a trader by *not* making the same mistakes as those who have failed. By studying hard, making it a business, implementing good trading habits (based on a solid method), and regulating the time you spend at it, you will definitely increase the odds in your favor.

When looking to other traders for advice, or information, do not allow their jargon to intimidate or mislead you. Unless the source has a proven track record of successful trading, you will probably be getting bad information anyway. Therefore, when developing your trading plan, try and draw information out of other traders based on what causes their losses. If the truth were to be told, the majority of traders have had more experience in losing money in the markets than they have had at making it. Therefore, why not utilize this information to your advantage?

It is not my intention to discourage the reader by revealing the fact that only those who are truly dedicated will make it in the real world as a trader (and subsequently avoid burnout). Rather, just the opposite is true. This information is provided to strengthen the reader's chances of success by hopefully motivating that trader to work hard at learning what really works by eliminating what doesn't, and then applying this understanding as it relates to the business of trading.

An unfortunate—but true—saying is that most successes are built on a multitude of failures. Therefore, it is this trader's opinion that it is more advantageous to learn, and therefore avoid, what causes losing trades rather than to focus on the multitude of readily available claims to riches that are constantly circulating, and which are here today and gone tomorrow.

As we cover the material in the following chapters, I will be using different terminology when referring to various aspects pertaining to the market. I intentionally do this in order to familiarize you with the different terms used by traders to convey the same thing. It can be very confusing in this business, because there is no unified standard dialect among traders. This is because each Guru that comes along changes different terms (for whatever reason, I don't really know).

An example of this is the A, B, C, a.k.a. P1, P2, P3. Another example of this would be cycle low, cycle high, a.k.a. turn point low, and turn point high. It just depends on who is speaking and what terminology he prefers. You don't want to hesitate to ask for clarification of a term being used. It would only be to your detriment not to do so, and you could miss out on beneficial information.

Before we get started on the charts and trade setups, I would like to cover some needed information. Many charting programs today have the ability to build different types of charts. Some examples would be volume, tick, minute, daily, weekly, monthly, yearly, etc.

If you are trading long-term, you would most likely want to use a daily or weekly chart. If you are trading short-term (day trading), you would use minute, tick, or volume charts. A tick chart is built on the amount of ticks you set the chart for, and does not work off of time.

Minute charts work off of time. Once the set increment of time has passed, the bar is completed.

Volume charts are based on the number of shares traded. For instance, if you had a volume chart set to 1500 share bars, once 1500 shares were traded on that market, then that bar would close and a new bar would start. Volume and tick charts have nothing to do with time. You could watch several minutes go by before 1500 shares were traded, or it could happen in a second.

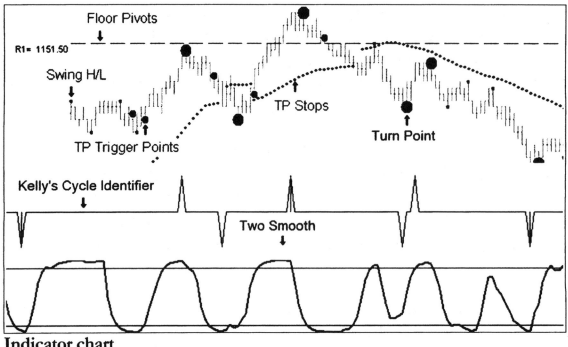

Indicator chart

This chart will help to identify the indicators being used on the charts. I have designed many custom indicators, and they work better than the standard ones that come with most software charting programs. However, you can still use the standard indicators to trade with if you prefer. Under Appendix B, there is a cross reference of indicators that are the closest comparisons to the custom ones I have developed.

The dashed lines that are shown across the chart are the floor pivots. The very small dots at the tops and bottoms are the swing high/low indicators. The larger dots above and below the cycle high and low are the turn point indicator. The indicator that looks like peaks and valleys is the Kelly's Cycle Identifier (Cycle Id). The dots that are above and below the price are my TrendPro Stop indicators and the oscillator at the bottom of the chart is a custom stochastic of mine called Two Smooth. As I review the trading charts, I will point out any new indicators used.

When viewing the following charts, keep in mind that some of the charts show actual trades. The reason why the entry may not match the exact entry based on our rules (found in Chapters 8 and 9), is because I used a market order for the entry. When you use a market order, there will most likely be some slippage. The entry price given would be the actual fill price. If the distance between P1 and P2 was not great enough to calculate the correct target, then I would generally use a 2.5:1 reward/risk ratio (because currently this is the ratio that I prefer). However, on some of the charts I used different ratios depending on market movement. I backed the target off by one tick. Depending on the volatility of the market being traded, I would use one tick or two ticks from P3 for the stop. I used a market order to enter the trade, a stop order for the stop, and a limit order for the profit target. The arrows you see on the charts point to *the bar* the order was filled on (not the exact price).

When reviewing the following chapters, should you be doing the math, you may find that your calculations differ somewhat from those given. This can happen very easily, as there are multiple variables. The objective in explaining the various trade setups is not to test the reader's math skill; but rather to familiarize the trader with the setups and the execution of the trades being shown. Additionally, the price on the chart may not always line up exactly with the numbers given in the paragraphs that review the trade. If you still feel compelled to work the numbers with a ruler (drawing a line on the prices on the charts), keep in mind that your line may not line up 100% of the time. A drawing tool was used for drawing some of the lines on the charts and is not 100% on the mark at times. For the most part, when I was calculating an entry and target for a short, I would round the entry price down to the nearest price, and the profit target was rounded up to the nearest price. For a long entry, I usually rounded the entry up to the closest price, and usually rounded the profit target down to the nearest price.

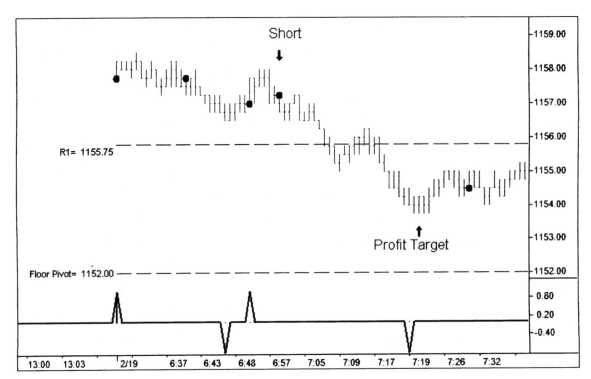

ES, 1500 Share Bar, February 19, 2004

The trades which I have included in the remainder of this book are intended to be used as teaching tools, and do not take into consideration exchange fees or commissions when calculating the profits or the losses.

The chart above is a 1500 share bar (volume bar). This chart shows the ES (S&P 500 E-mini) trade setup on the morning of February 19, 2004. The indicator on the bottom of the chart is the Kelly's Cycle Identifier. It calls out price movements based on what was covered in Chapter 6. The dashed lines across the chart are the floor pivot and floor resistance areas based on what was covered in Chapter 11. The dots on the price are from my indicator called TrendPro Trigger Points. This is a custom indicator I designed to trigger an entry.

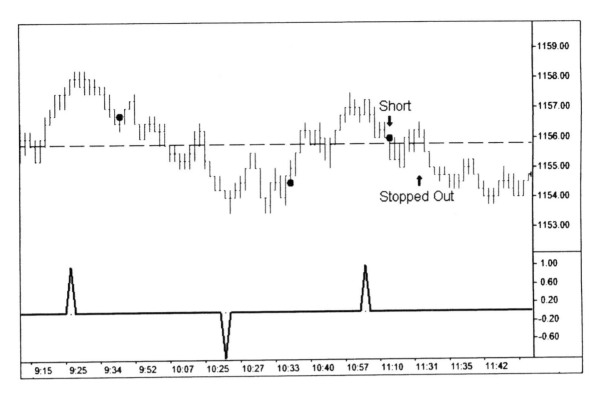

ES, 1500 Share Bar, February 19, 2004

This chart is a prototype of a short trade based on the A, B, C setup. I have included this chart to illustrate the importance of staying with your trading plan and using good stop placements. The scenario for many traders would most likely go something like this: the trade was entered at 1155.75. The target was two points based on the current price movement between turn points.

Had the stop been placed where it should have been (just above the last swing high), this would have been a good trade; however, the stop was placed at 1156.75, which was too close, resulting in the trade getting stopped out. This is an all too common mistake. On the following charts, I will use one to two ticks from P3 for the stop.

Making mistakes is a skill that most of us are born with (traders not excluded); the key is to try and make as few of them as possible. This particular mistake, which I have observed many times over, is shown here to once again bring home the importance of staying with your trading plan and always using good stop placements.

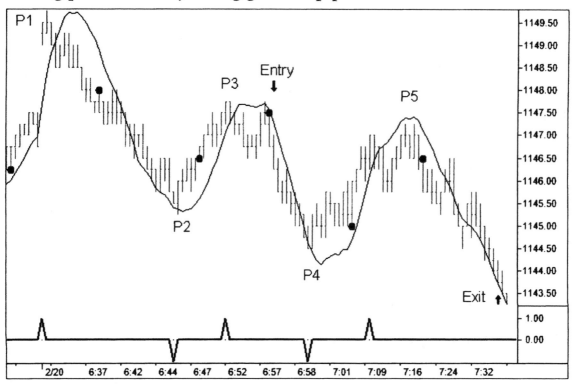

ES, 1500 Share Bar, February 20, 2004

Here the market gapped up on the open, the price came close to the floor pivot area at 1150.25, and then sold off. On the rally back, the price could not take out the high of P1 (turn point one), setting up the short at P3 (turn point three). This is a short based on the P1, P2, and P3 (as covered in Chapter 9). The indicators used were the floor pivots (not shown on this chart), Kelly's Cycle Identifier, Kelly's Advanced Moving Average (the line on the price), and my Trigger Points custom indicator (the dots on the chart).

The trade was entered at 1146.75 and closed (exited) at 1143.75. Using a three point profit target, this trade would have grossed 150.00 per contract before commissions. At the time of the writing of this book, one point in the ES was worth 50.00.

The trade on the previous page was one that most traders would have exited when P4 (turn point four) was forming. This is where discipline comes in. As I have previously explained, if a trader has a good set of rules that work the greater percentage of the time, then there would be no reason to panic should the trade not immediately go in his favor. I have seen this over and over again: it is called FEAR. Fear rears its ugly head because the trader doesn't have a proven set of rules in the first place; therefore, he gets whatever consolation he can by convincing himself of all the reasons the trade is not going in his direction right away. This type of trader fits the profile of *Trigger-Happy Clyde*. Should *Clyde* continue to trade in this manner, he will eventually (to his dismay) become gun-shy.

Most unsuccessful traders have acquired a measure of expertise at making excuses. I have been in many chat rooms (Advisory Services) on the net where the "advisor" will say, "The market is not moving fast enough in my direction. It's been six bars and the price isn't moving", or "I see buyers coming into the market" (being short in the market). Let me make this very clear—this type of trader won't last long. His rules are NOT solid, and they DON'T work most of the time. And if they don't work most of the time, then you will no doubt hear similar reason(s) to the ones mentioned above.

Here's another point to remember: If for any reason your stop is taken out (stopped out of the trade) and you get another setup, don't be afraid to take it. This is about the only thing that usually goes wrong with the P1, P2, and P3 setup. For instance, let's say I enter a trade and P3 doesn't hold, my stop is hit, and the price never moves past P1. The prudent course of action at this point would be to re-enter the trade on the next swing.

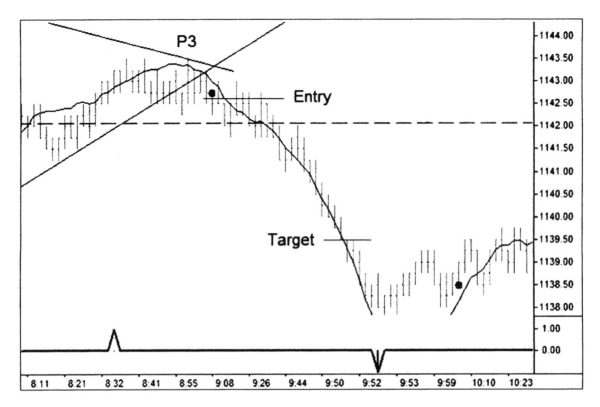

ES, 1500 Share Bar, February 20, 2004

This is another short setup based on a few different indicators not shown on the previous charts. I drew a trend line down from the previous swing highs (swing highs of three). I used the Kelly's Cycle Identifier for P1. I drew a trend line up based on previous swing lows (swing lows of three). The price broke the trend line up, the price was below the Kelly's Advanced Moving Average, and then the Trigger Points triggered the entry. This trade used the normal P1, P2, and P3 setup of the continuation of a trend trade.

The market was still in a downtrend at the time the setup was occurring, the price reversed, forming P2, rallied up above the support one area and ran out of steam, and then formed P3. This means that the rally was not strong enough to cause a reversal in the market to the long side. Confirming the short, the market broke below the support area at 1142.25, thus continuing the downtrend.

The entry price was 1142.50, the profit target was 1139.50. The price moved down reaching the target for three points.

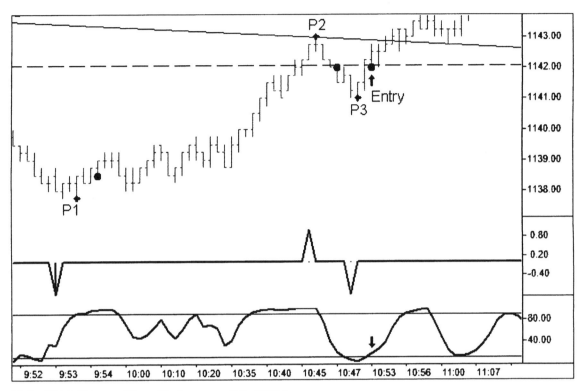

ES, 1500 Share Bar, February 20, 2004

This trade will be shown over two charts because the price had more movement than usual. The stochastic at the bottom of the chart is my custom Two Smooth.

On this chart, P1 was a major bottom as shown by the Kelly's Cycle Identifier (the line in the middle of the valley). This is referred to by some as the spike. Therefore, when the price broke above support one; I was looking for a long rather than a short, because the price movement from P1 to P2 was about six points. Once P2 was formed, I drew a trend line down from the last swing high. The P3 was identified by the Kelly's Cycle Identifier. The oscillator then broke above the oversold line, the Trigger Points triggered the long entry, and the price broke above the support area. At this point there was adequate confirmation for a long entry. To confirm the trade, the price broke above the trend line. The break above the trend line is where the majority of traders would have entered the trade; however, by this time sufficient confirmation for the entry had already taken place. The trend line break would have provided further confirmation on the direction of the current trend.

The chart below will show the completion of the trade.

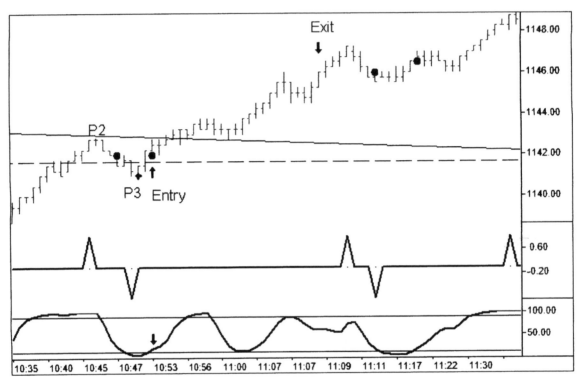

ES Chart, 1500 Share Bar, February 20, 2004

The long entry occurred at 1142.50. The profit target was 1145.50, and thus the profit would have been three points per contract. Trading one contract would result in a profit of 150.00 minus commissions.

As you can see, the market continued moving up after the target was achieved. This upsets some traders, and they say, "Look at all the money I left on the table." The problem with this reasoning is this:

Moves like that happen very rarely. If you are having difficulty in this area, let me suggest doing one of the following: re-enter the trade on the next swing low (if it meets your trade setup), or trade multiple contracts and take profit on the majority of them at your profit target and let a few run. I would also move my stop to break-even, plus a tick to cover commissions (or use a trailing stop). I like using a fixed stop, as this helps eliminate human error.

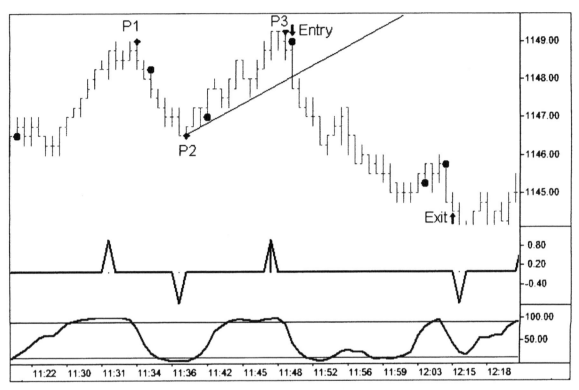

ES Chart, 1500 Share Bar, February 20, 2004

This trade had a lot going for it. Right above P1 and P3 was the floor pivot at 1150.25. P3 was less in value than the high at P1 (meaning the close of the bar to the right of the high at P3). The Two Smooth stochastic broke below the overbought area, the Trigger Points triggered, and at the same time, a trend line was broken.

The entry price was 1147.75, the profit target was 1144.75, and I would have placed the stop at 1149.50. I would have risked 1.75

points with a target of three points. This trade would have grossed three points before commissions.

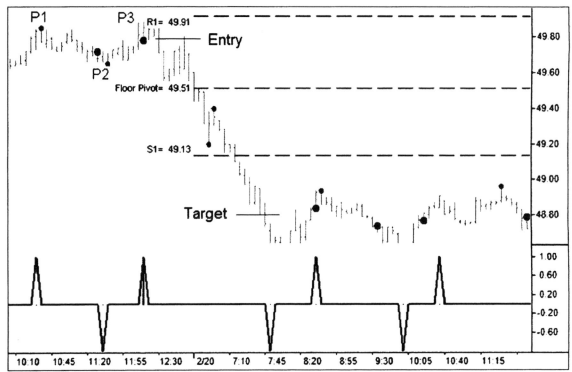

GM, 5 Minute Chart, February 20, 2004

This is a five minute GM (General Motors) chart. I wanted to show that the basic setup works on all time frames and all freely traded markets. The P1 and P2 occurred on February 19, 2004, and the P3 formed before the close of the same day. There are two ways to trade this: A trader could have shorted GM on the setup at P3 and held the position overnight, or the trade could have been entered a few minutes after the opening on February 20, 2004 on a retest of the floor resistance at 49.91.

The entry would have been in the 49.80 area, and the target for this trade would have been set in the 48.70 area. The trade would have been good for one point. Had a trader been trading ten thousand shares that would have resulted in a gross profit of 10,000.00.

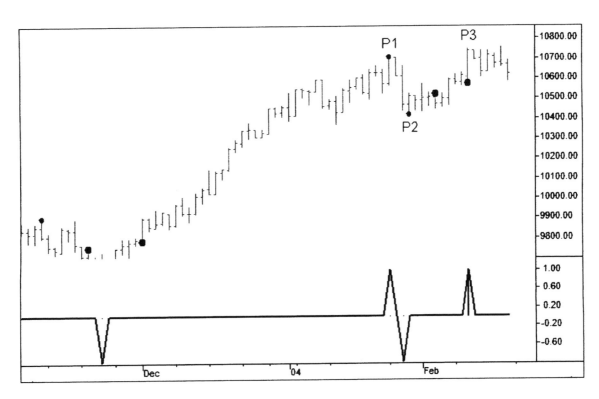

INDU Chart, daily, February 20, 2004

This is an INDU (Dow Jones) daily chart. We have a P1, P2, and P3 forming on the above Dow chart, with P3 not yet confirmed. Based on what we see here, the market may well be headed down. The next chart will show how it turned out.

INDU Chart, daily, May 18, 2004

The setup to sell worked out great. The confirming price for the market to sell off was 10581.55, reaching a low on March 24, 2004 of 10007.49. The market rallied back up to the 10600.00 area, then sold off again, going below 10000.00 to 9852.19 on May 12, 2004.

Anyone using my method could have exited their long positions, and then would have done one of these two things: Wait until the market developed a setup for a long entry, or short the market based on a continuation of the downtrend.

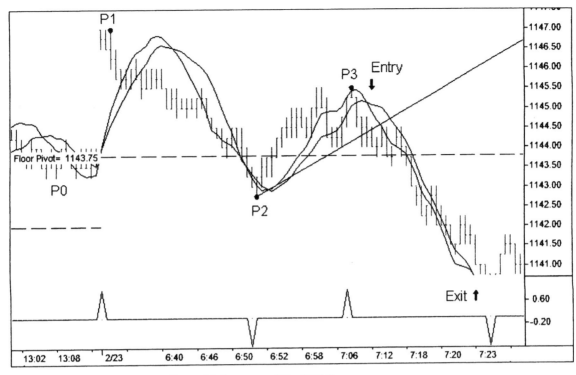

ES Chart, 1500 Share Bar, February 23, 2004

I am going to show quite a few different indicators to both confirm and enter a trade. This way you will get a better feel for the ones you may want to use. In the above chart, I used the Kelly's Cycle Identifier (the one at the bottom of the screen). The dots above and below the turn points are plotted from the Kelly's Turn Point indicator. The dashed lines across the screen are the floor pivots, and the line that extends up from P2 is a trend line. The two lines moving with the price are moving averages (in this screen shot I used my Kelly's Advanced Moving Average).

This was a great setup; however, let's review how most traders would have traded this. The first way would have been to sell the breakout below the floor pivot at 1143.75. The second way would have been to buy after P2 formed on the breakout above the floor pivot. The trader who sold the breakout below the floor pivot would have lost money, and it would be doubtful that the trader buying the breakout above the floor pivot would have made much—if anything.

On the other hand, an alert trader such as *Ready Freddy* would have seen that P2 was less in value than P0, and therefore, would not have taken the long breakout above the floor pivot. He knew that because P2 was less in value than P0 (P0 is the previous low turn point before P2), as a rule, P3 would start a reversal to the downside. Also because P3 was less than P1, *Freddy* would have determined that this setup met the conditions of his trading plan. After P3 formed, there were two triggers to enter the short; the first was the moving average crossover, and secondly, the trend line up was broken on the same price bar. The entry price was 1144.25, the stop was 1145.75, and the target was 1141.25. Once the price broke the floor pivot, *Freddy* would have had more confirmation that the trade was going in his favor. The market moved on down and the profit target was attained.

For an explanation of what the different "P" numbers represent, please refer to Chapter 12 (Reviewing Trend).

You should make an effort to remember which indicators are which as you go through the charts, because later I may not refer to them by name. At this point, you should be able to start recognizing them. If I use something new or different, then I will point it out.

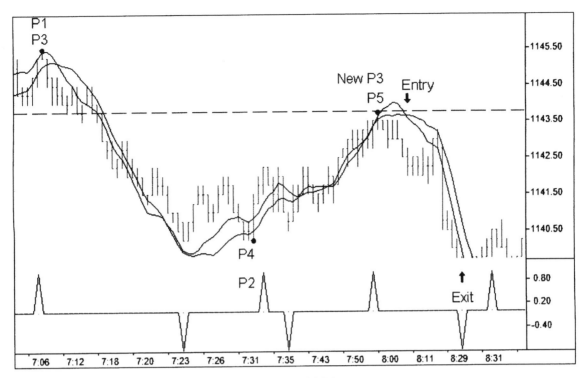

ES Chart, 1500 Share Bar, February 23, 2004

This chart may seem confusing at first due to the numbering of the turn points. Some traders will label them P1, P2, P3, P4, P5, and so on as the trend continues. This can get confusing. That is why I prefer to move my P1, P2, and P3 forward to the next setup, rather than carrying the count forward. This is a continuation of the previous chart. The old P3 becomes the new P1 as the setup develops, and the P4 above (where our last target was) becomes P2. The old P5 then would become the new P3. In the future, I will just refer to them as A, B, C or P1, P2, and P3. You will want to label the chart(s) in the manner most suitable for you. The main thing is that you identify and keep track of them for trading purposes.

The same indicators were used on this chart as on the previous one. This was as good as it gets. The price went up and tested the floor pivot at 1143.75. The price couldn't move above it, so the floor pivot became resistance. Once my Kelly's Advanced Moving Average crossed over the other Kelly's Advanced Moving Average (with a different length setting), it triggered the short entry at 1142.25. The stop was a quarter of a point above the floor pivot. The stop was 1144.00. The profit target was 1139.25, the market sold off, and the profit was reached.

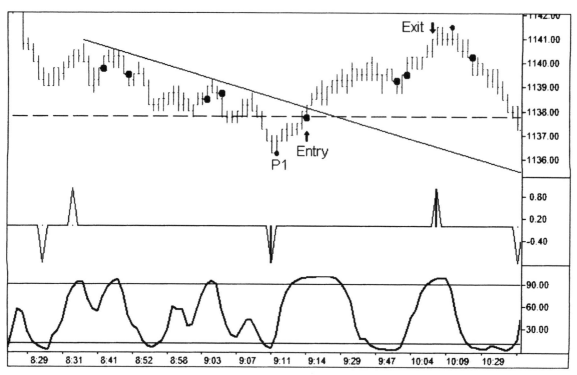

ES Chart, 1500 Share Bar, February 23, 2004

The trade setup illustrated above is a higher risk type of trade and should be left for the advanced trader(s). However, as you grow in your trading skills, it may be one you would want to add to your trading plan.

Because this is a higher risk trade, an additional amount of confirmation would be required. This is why I added an oscillator (my custom Two Smooth stochastic), and the TrendPro Trigger Points (one of my custom indicators). The price broke below support one at 1137.75, but did not sell off quickly; rather, buyers came in and the market rallied above the support area.

The Cycle Identifier plotted showing a major turn point. Also, the custom Two Smooth stochastic broke above the oversold area, and the price broke the trend line down. At the same time, the Trigger Points gave the entry signal.

Entry was at 1138.25, the stop was placed just below P1 at 1136.00, and the target was placed at 1141.25. The price moved in the direction of the trade and the profit target was realized.

Some traders will take less of a profit on a counter trend trade, such as this one. I am not recommending counter trend trading; in fact, I would not recommend counter trend trading to anyone.

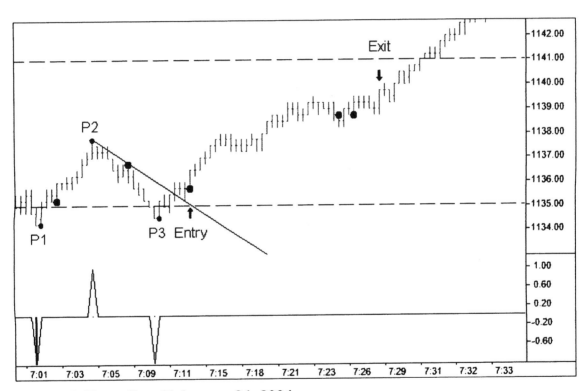

ES, 1500 Share Bar, February 24, 2004

Here we had a major cycle at P1 (the spike in the center of the valley) on the Kelly's Cycle Identifier. The market found support at 1135.00, and then the price rallied some. P2 was formed after the market sold off back down to support one. P3 was located with the Kelly's Cycle Identifier, and then broke a trend line, and the TrendPro Trigger Points plotted the entry at 1136.50. The stop was 1134.50, and the target was 1139.50. The market moved up and the profit target was reached.

I have observed that traders who share *Trigger-Happy Clyde's* personality traits would have jumped out of the trade on the pullback you see at the 1139.00 price area. They would have done this just because a few indicators had turned down. Once again FEAR (being the father of failure) would cause this to happen; making it clear that the trader didn't believe his setup was based on solid ground. If you have a solid plan that works the greater percentage of the time, then this would not happen and like *Ready Freddy,* you would stay in the trade until you reached your target. Let me again stress this point: Have a plan, make sure it works the majority of the time, and trade the plan.

I am trying to keep the charts very clean (meaning very few indicators). *Slow Moe* would need the chart filled full of indicators, so many in fact, that it would take all day to review a chart. On the other hand, *Trigger- Happy Clyde* would be saying, "I can trade without any indicators." *Ready Freddy* already knows what indicators to use, because it is part of his trading plan, thereby eliminating the stress of last minute decisions, which would happen to *Slow Moe*—or the angst that *Trigger-Happy Clyde* would be experiencing after blowing out his trading account.

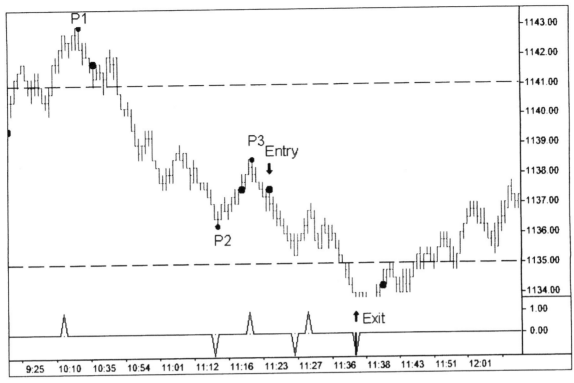

ES, 1500 Share Bar, February 24, 2004

This trade was a little different as we didn't have a dominant (major) cycle at P1; but, from P1 the market sold off rather quickly, retraced a little, and formed P3. The entry was triggered with the Trigger Points indicator giving the short entry at 1137.00. The stop was placed at 1138.75, and the profit target was placed at 1134.00.

This would have made even the best of the best trader nervous about reaching the target; however, you need to stay with your trading plan. When the price reached the floor pivot, most traders would have been exiting the trade and entering long, or going flat (closing out of their position). However, staying with the predetermined set of rules, the profit objective was met, and the price did go down to the profit target.

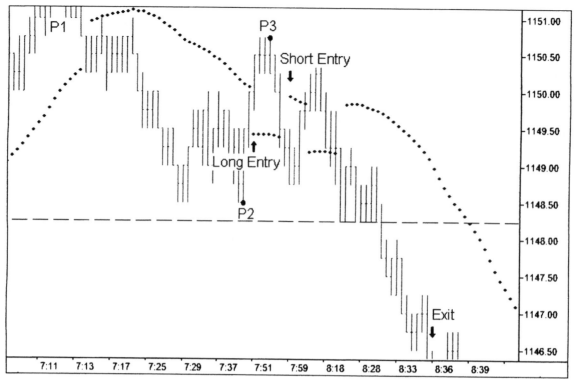

ES, 1500 Share Bar, February 27, 2004

This chart illustrates a rather strange trading day. It was very choppy (no real consistency in price action). There was a setup for a long in the direction of the trend. The entry looked even better than normal because price turned close to the resistance at 1148.50. P3 formed, and the trade was entered long at 1149.50, the stop was 1148.25, and the target was 1152.50. Shortly after entering the long trade, the market set up for a reversal to the downside. The short was entered at 1149.25, the stop for the short was placed at 1150.75, and the profit target was placed at 1146.25. Chapter 10 gives more clarification in regard to the different ways to trade a reversal.

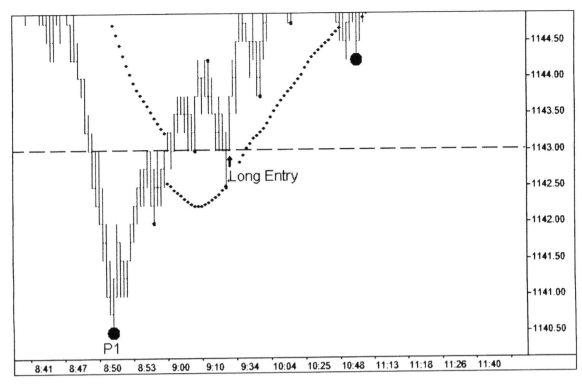

ES, 1500 Share Bar, February 27, 2004

I removed the Kelly's Cycle Identifier from the subgraph in the above chart in order to show the trade; however, I am still using it to identify P1. On this chart we didn't have a Cycle Identifier plot for the P2 showing because it didn't meet the qualification. As the market was very choppy on this particular day, I was using a swing high/swing low indicator (the smaller dots on the swings). The price came down to the floor pivot at 1143.00, broke a little below it, then came back up and bounced around it—showing that there was support in this area. Entering long at 1143.00, the stop would have been placed at 1142.25, and the profit target would have been placed at 1145.25. The price did go up to reach the target.

This type of trade is very common among traders. The price broke above the floor pivot and came back down for a retest, couldn't break below it, so it became a support area. Keep in mind, this is a high risk type of trade and careful study needs to be made before trading this type of pattern.

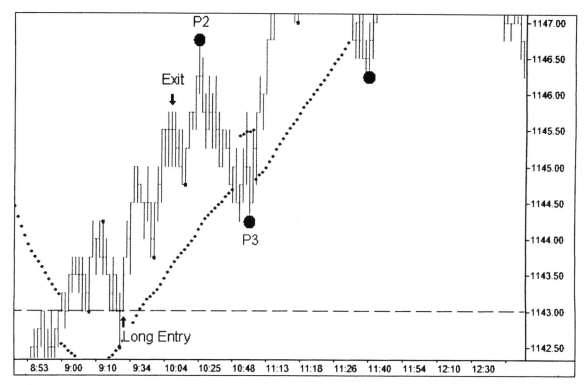

ES, 1500 Share Bar, February 27, 2004

This chart shows the entry for the long and the profit target from the previous chart. This type of trade is very aggressive. In my opinion, a better strategy would be to wait for the P2 and P3 to form based on what we covered in Chapter 8. Even if you would have taken the more aggressive trade, you still could have entered a trade off of the normal P1, P2, and P3 setup. The smaller dots on the swings are the swing high/swing low indicator covered in Chapter 5. The larger dots are from the turn point indicator also covered in Chapter 5.

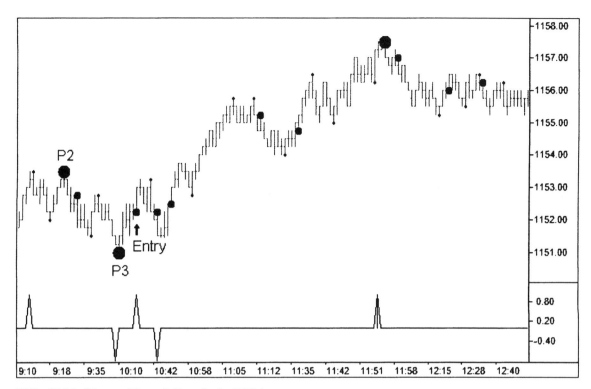

ES, 1500 Share Bar, March 1, 2004

On this chart, I confirmed P1 with the Kelly's Cycle Identifier, and P2 was confirmed with the turn point indicator. The Trigger Points triggered an entry at 1153.00 and the stop was placed at 1150.75. The profit target was placed at 1158.00. The market moved up to 1157.00 and then started going sideways (no range in price). Being close to the end of the day, it would be common to place a MOC order (market order on close). However, I suggest exiting the trade a few minutes before the close.

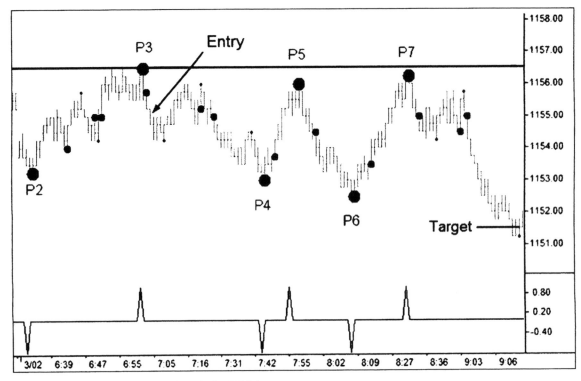

ES, 1500 Share Bar, March 2, 2004

There is a lot to be learned from this chart. A P1 was formed from the day before, and then P2 was confirmed with the turn points. P3 was located with the Kelly's Cycle Identifier, and the short entry was triggered using the Trigger Points. The entry was 1155.25, the stop was placed at 1156.75, and the profit target was placed at 1151.50. The market moved down and the profit was taken later in the day.

Correct placement of the stop above P3 would be crucial. As you can see, the market tested the floor resistance several times before selling off. If a trader, such as *Trigger-Happy Clyde,* would have been trading this, panic would have set in at P4. *Clyde* would panic because the profit target was not reached, and the market started heading up. *Clyde* would have tried to go long, then short again at P5, then would have entered long at P6, and then shorted again at P7. *Clyde* would have been going crazy, and subsequently, be no richer for the wear. On the other hand, *Ready Freddy* knows his trading plan, his winning average, and trades his plan. *Ready Freddy* would have stayed in the trade until one of two things happened: Either he would have gotten stopped out, or his profit target would have been reached. The reason for his staying in the trade is this: He knew how often he would win, and he knew he had a solid set of trading rules. This is, by far, a better and easier way to trade. We do not want to leave out *Slow Moe,* who would still be reviewing so many different methods and indicators that no trade would have ever been taken.

At my seminars I often ask this question to the attendees, "How many here know your percentage of winning trades?" Their responses reveal that only about twenty percent have taken the time to keep a record of their trades. This is unfortunate, as this is the very foundation that a trader needs to build from. If you do not have a solid foundation, then how can you build on it? You need to be able to recognize, and change, whatever it is that may be hindering your success as a trader.

Money management is the secret to success in this business, and that includes knowing your percentage of winning trades.

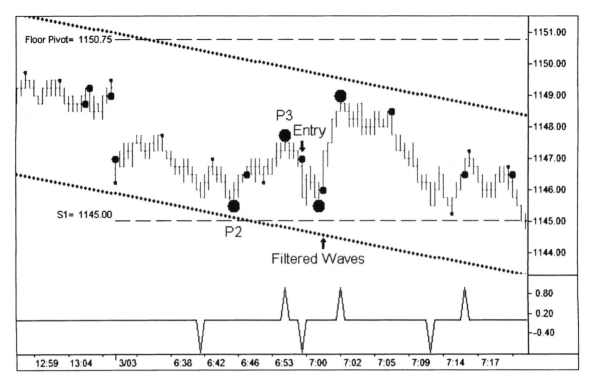

ES, 1500 Share Bar, March 3, 2004

Due to the choppiness of the market, I added an additional indicator to this chart. This indicator helps to identify trend and is called Filtered Waves (one of my custom indicators, and is available as part of one of my indicator packages). As you study the charts throughout these chapters, you will notice I use different indicators, and switch back and forth between them. This is because some indicators work better in a particular type of market condition than do others.

On this chart, the P1 for the setup was from the previous day. The market gapped down on the opening, and then P2 formed. Once P3 was confirmed for a short, the entry would have been 1145.75. The market then rallied up hitting the stop at 1148.25, with a loss of 2.5 points.

This is an example of a setup that should be avoided. The reason being is that the stop was too large from the entry price and the market did not have enough price movement to justify a 2.5:1

reward/risk ratio. When we take into consideration that the stop was about 2.5 points from the entry price, we realize that there was no room for profit with a 3.0 target. It's called getting in late (chasing the trade), and this is why the win/loss ratio is so important. If you were only winning 50% of the time, and your stop was the same as your profit target, you would be losing money. Seeing that the market had already moved three points, you would have avoided the trade and waited for the next one.

The importance of knowing your win/loss ratio becomes even more evident in regards to the calculations needed in determining how large the profit target needs to be in comparison to the stop. Let's say, for instance, that your win/loss percent ratio was 60/40. If that were the case, then your stop could be about the same as your target. I am not necessarily recommending that. Rather, I am trying to show the essentials of managing a trade, and the significance of knowing your win/loss ratio.

Nothing works 100% of the time, and the only constant is that you *will* have losing trades. However, if you use good money management, have a trading plan (set of rules), and know your win/loss ratio, then—and only then—will you make money trading with consistency.

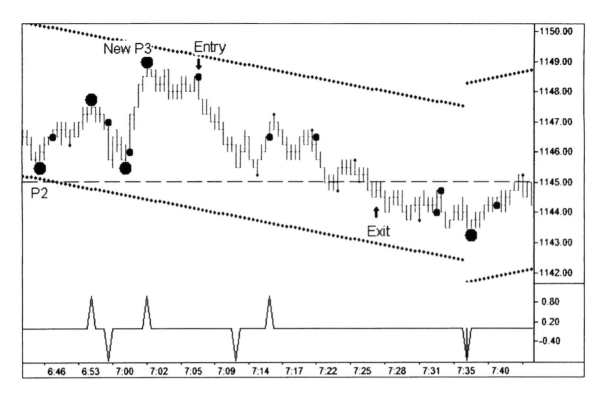

ES, 1500 Share Bar, March 3, 2004

As you have probably noticed, this is a continuation of the chart from the last trade. A new P3 formed, and the entry was 1147.75, and the stop was placed at 1149.00. The price came down to reach the profit target at 1144.75, and the trade resulted in a profit of 3 points. To clarify when I talk about points, I am basing my calculations on one contract. If you were trading 100 contracts, that would be 300 points, but still only 3 points per contract.

So far on this trading day (after commissions) a trader would have, at best, broken even. Remember, as I have said before, it is vital to take all the trades, and re-enter if you get stopped out. If the trade had not been re-entered, it would have resulted in a loss of 2.50 points; however, because of the re-entry the trader would be at break-even.

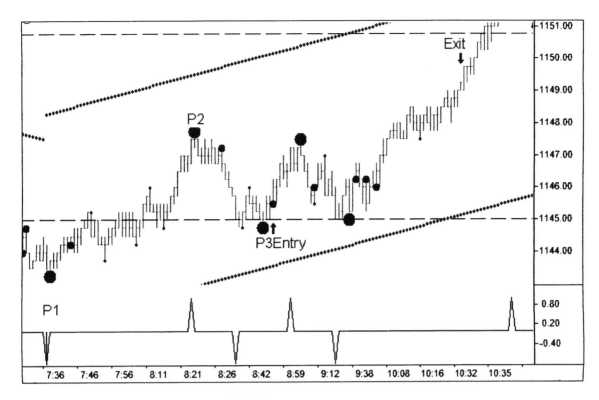

ES, 1500 Share Bar, March 3, 2004

For the last trade of the day, I had a major spike (major cycle bottom) pin-pointed by the Kelly's Cycle Identifier. The price broke above floor support at 1145.00, and then P2 was confirmed by the Turn Point indicator. The price retested support, P3 formed, and I had a trigger to enter long from the Trigger Points. The entry was 1146.00, and the stop was placed at 1144.50. The market rallied up, and the profit target was reached.

So for this day, if all three trades would have been taken, the gross profit would have been 2.5 points. At first this does not sound like much money; however, had twenty contracts been traded, the profit would increase to 2,500.00—not bad for a day's work.

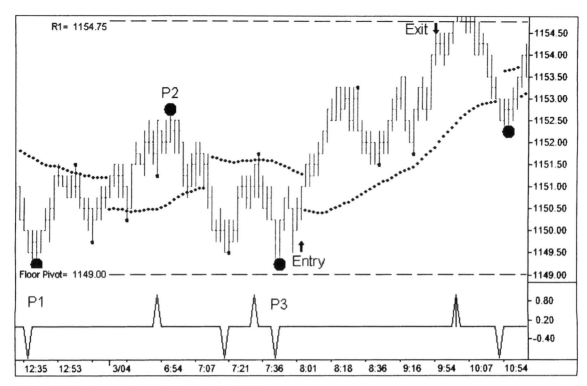

ES, 3000 Share Bar, March 4, 2004

At the time of this trade the market range had become very small, about 6.5 points for the day. Any time the price range narrows, the market becomes harder to trade; subsequently, I moved out to a larger chart and started using a 3,000 share bar chart (volume bar) to try and cut down on the noise (choppiness of the market). P1 and P2 were confirmed with both the Kelly's Cycle Identifier, and the Turn Points indicator. P3 was identified with the Kelly's Cycle Identifier, and tested the floor pivot area at 1149.00.

The entry was triggered with the TrendPro Stops at 1151.00, and the stop was placed at 1149.00. The price went right up and reached the profit target, and then moved a little higher and tested the resistance one area. For the most part, the market went sideways the rest of the day.

Remember: If the chart (time frame) you are trading becomes un-tradable, move to a time frame that *is* tradable.

CHAPTER 15

The Real World

∙∙∙

Trading Real-time—Real Money

"*P*eople are their own worst enemy," so the saying goes. In the real world of trading, traders need to be willing to take responsibility for their own mistakes. Being accountable for our own mistakes will rule out passing the blame on to others in the industry. We live in a world where everyone blames someone, or something else, rather than owning up to their own actions. This can distract us from addressing the real issue—which would be to identify whatever problem or difficulty we may be experiencing and correct it. The moral of the story: Those who shrink from responsibility keep on shrinking in other ways, too (i.e. their trading account). Do your homework. Pay your dues before putting your hard earned money on the line. If you don't, you would do better going to Las Vegas and playing the slot machines or aimlessly throwing darts at a stock market dartboard. Be willing to learn from other traders' mistakes, as most likely you won't live long enough to make them all yourself. The biggest mistake-making culprits in regard to trading are lack of understanding, lack of proper training, and/or unwillingness to learn from others.

You may have heard the saying, "Those who can…do, and those who can't …teach." Or, in this business it could be rephrased, "Those who can …do, and those who can't…sell software." Perhaps we can ask the question: In the absence of those selling software, would we be seeing such a large number of individuals who are trading the markets currently? The answer would be No! There wouldn't be. For the most part, these vendors perform a great service. Like with any business though, there is both good and bad. When choosing trading software, rather than responding to hype and large ads, look for merchants that have been around long enough to have built a good reputation, or come as a referral. It is my opinion, that if you are looking to purchase trading indicators, or systems, or perhaps an advisory service, you would want to deal exclusively with vendors that have a good reputation. Also, it would be wise not to buy into hype or high-pressure sales.

Here is another pointer: Approach trading and investing as a business (for profit activity), not as a hobby (pastime activity), and you will do fine.

Chart Patterns and Trading Techniques

Keep in mind, the method shown in the following examples work on all time frames, and all freely traded markets. It doesn't matter whether you are trading stocks, futures, currencies, options, or mutual funds—they all trade about the same. Additionally, it doesn't matter what the time frame is. Whether it is an intraday, daily, weekly, or monthly chart, the setup works the same. Therefore, there is no need to become troubled over the fact that most of the charts in this book show either the ES (S&P 500 E-mini) or ER2 (Russell 2000 E-mini).

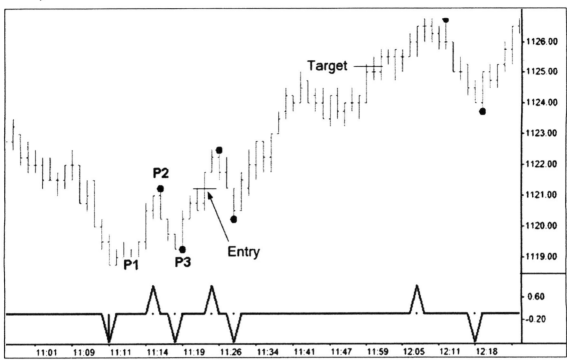

ES, 3000 Share Bar, March 15, 2004

This was a nice and easy setup for recognizing P1, P2, and P3. The entry price would have been 1120.75, and the stop would have been placed at 1118.50. The profit target was placed at 1125.25, which was calculated using a 2:1 reward/risk ratio. This trade would have grossed 4.50 points.

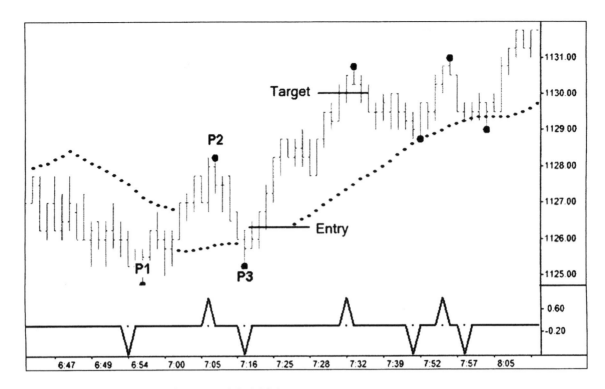

ES, 3000 Share Bar, March 16, 2004

P1=1124.75, P2=1128.25, and P3=1125.25. The stop would have been placed at 1124.75, the entry was 1126.25, and the profit target was 1130.00 using a 2.5:1 ratio, for a gross profit of 3.75 points. I would have given up 1.5 points if the trade went against me.

If I had real money on the line, I would have been looking for some other strong indication(s) that the trade would go in a positive direction. To feel confident about the trade, I would have needed floor or Fibonacci support from other indicators. I would have been looking for a major bottom at P1 (which was not the case).

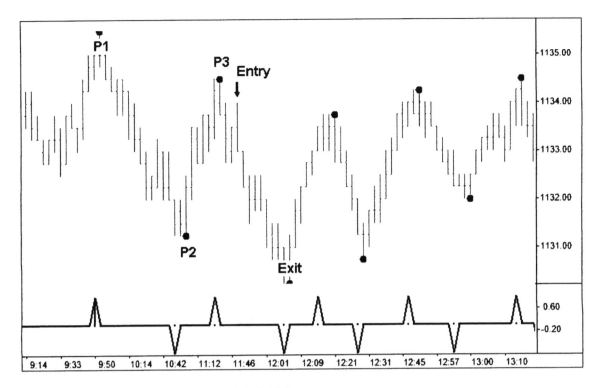

ES, 3000 Share Bar, March 16, 2004

To keep this chart very clean and simple, I am only using two indicators, the Kelly's Cycle Identifier at the bottom, and my turn points.

P1=1135.50, P2=1131.25, and P3=1134.50. Based on this, my entry was 1133.25, the profit target was placed at 1130.50, and the stop was placed at 1135.00. Based on the information covered in Chapter 9, under the subtitle *Short Profit Target*, I backed my target off by one tick in order to stay in the 25% range of taking profit.

It is amazing that if you don't use a profit target (limit order), more often than not, the market will reverse right on your price and you won't be able to get a fill. In the above example, the market went right to 1130.25. This would have been another profitable trade.

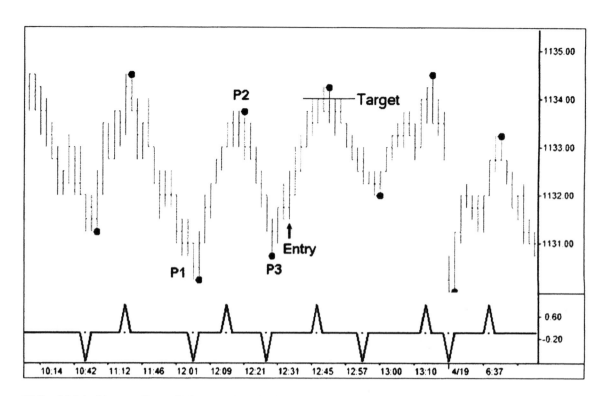

ES, 3000 Share Bar, March 16, 2004

P1=1130.25, P2=1133.75, and P3=1130.75. The entry price was 1131.75, the stop was placed at 1130.25, and the profit target was placed at 1134.00. The market moved up, the target was realized.

If the market had gone against us, we would have lost 1.5 points, compared to a profit of 2.25.

I have been keeping the charts very simple. We could, and should, be using more indicators for better confirmation; however, it's clear that this method (though not complex) works. Sometimes a simple approach works best in trading—as well as in other aspects of life.

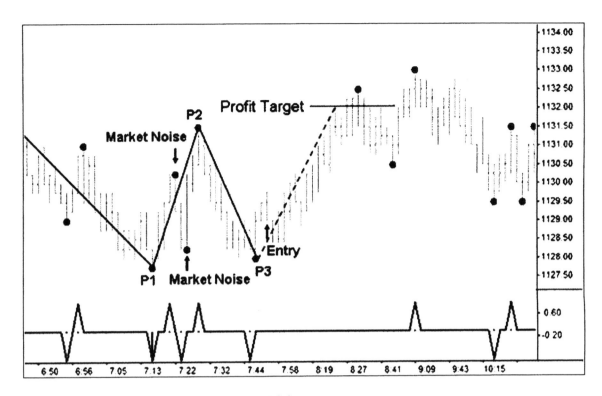

ES, 3000 Share Bar, March 19, 2004

This is a chart you will want to examine carefully. We can learn a great deal from this setup. As I covered in earlier chapters, using a filter is an invaluable tool that can prevent many losing trades (notice the noise between P1 and P2).

P1=1127.75, P2=1131.50, and P3=1128.00. The entry price was 1129.00 and the stop was placed at 1127.50. The profit target was calculated using a 2:1 reward/risk ratio and was placed at 1132.00. This was another profitable setup.

In case you were wondering why the dates on the charts are from different months rather than consecutive days—the reason is that I only used charts from the days I was writing the book.

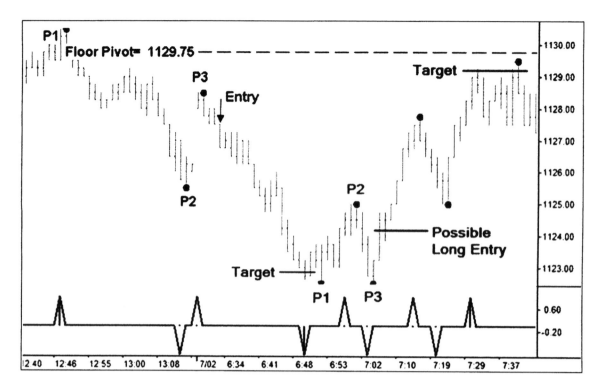

ES, 3000 Share Bar, July 2, 2004

This is definitely a chart to study. If you remember, in the previous chapters I mentioned that the P1 and P2 could be from the day before. This chart shows such an example. P1=1130.50, P2=1125.50, and P3=1128.50. The entry was 1127.25, the stop was placed at 1129.00, and the profit target was placed at 1123.75. There was added confirmation on this short setup, as the market gapped up but couldn't take out the floor pivot at 1129.75. The market sold off in the needed direction to reach the profit target.

The market then formed a major bottom, tested the bottom again, (thus we had a double bottom) and our P1, P2, and P3 were in place. After P3 was confirmed, a trader could have entered long; however, it most likely would have been a late entry at 1124.25 making the stop loss 2.5 points. Now it's true that the distance between P1 and P2 didn't meet our filter; however, when we take into consideration the double bottom (and that we had a 3.50 point profit from the short), even if the long did go against us, we would have risked nothing. As it worked out, the long worked in our favor reaching the target at 1129.25. I was unable to use the normal formula for the target because there were only 2.75 points between P1 and P2. I used a 2.0:1 reward/risk ratio for the target to keep it at a minimum of two times my stop loss. The reason for the 2.0:1 reward/risk is because there was already a winning trade, and the price sold off the floor pivot early.

A stop for the long would have been placed at 1121.75 (a 2.5 point risk from the long entry price of 1124.25). When considering where the profit target needed to be placed, I took into consideration the Floor Pivot at 1129.75 and that the market had sold off that price earlier.

Bear in mind, I am not saying that a long position should have been taken. I am only pointing out how some advanced and/or aggressive traders may have traded it. There is no shame in walking away with a gross profit of 3.50 points per contract.

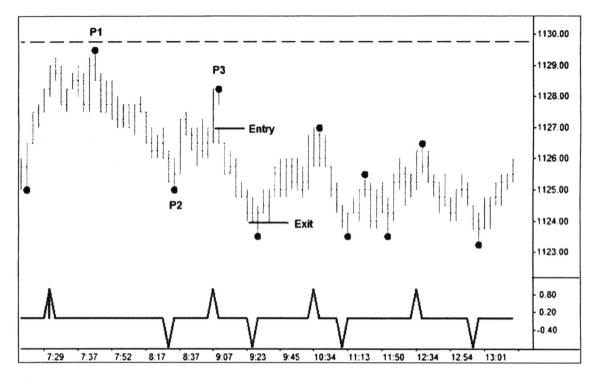

ES, 3000 Share Bar, July 2, 2004

P1=1129.50, P2=1125.00, and P3=1128.25. The dashed line at the top of the chart is the floor pivot at 1129.75. The market rallied up testing the floor pivot, and then formed P1, sold off some, and formed P2. After P2 was confirmed, we started looking for P3, and shorted at 1127.00. The stop was placed at 1128.75, and the profit target was placed at 1124.00. The market sold off, reaching the target for a nice 3 point profit.

Although this turned out to be a good trade, it would have been one that we would want to steer clear of. I included it for illustration purposes to explain why it should not have been taken. The reason we would have passed on taking this trade is because it did not meet our reward/risk ratio of 2.5:1, and the market did not have enough price movement to warrant adjusting our target to meet our 2.5:1 ratio. We had a 1.75 point stop, and a 3 point profit target. Remember what we learned earlier—the target needs to be greater than our stop, and we need at least a 2.5:1 ratio (of course that ratio could be adjusted, depending on the win/loss ratio). A good rule is about 2.5:1. There is no hard rule on this—it really comes down to the trader, and that trader's rules.

To trade with a 2.5:1 ratio (reward/risk), you would need to be trading with a win/loss ratio of better than 40/60. In other words, if your stop was 1 point, your profit target should be about 2.5 points (with a 40/60 win/loss ratio).

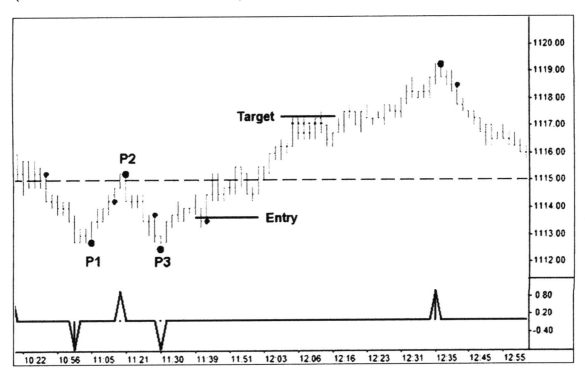

ES, 3000 Share Bar, July 6, 2004

P1=1112.75, P2=1115.25, and P3=1112.50. The dashed line across the chart is floor support at 1115.00. This is a bit on the aggressive side of trading. We had a major P1, and then P2 formed, and we had a double bottom. We added another indicator (TrendPro Trigger Points), which is a custom indicator I designed to help verify the entry. The entry was at 1113.50 due to slippage. The stop was placed at 1112.00. Because there wasn't enough price movement between P1 and P2 to calculate a good profit target, I used 3.75 points. The profit objective was met as the market moved up to the profit target at 1117.25.

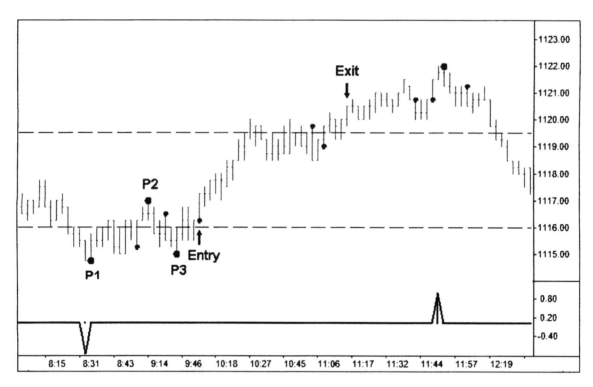

ES, 3000 Share Bar, July 7, 2004

P1=1114.75, P2=1117.00, and P3=1115.00. The dashed line at 1116.00 is the floor pivot, and the dashed line at 1119.50 is resistance. This is another aggressive type of trade. However, we did have a P1, and then P2, and the price was finding support at the floor pivot. The entry price was 1116.25, the stop was placed at 1114.50, and the profit target was placed at 1120.50. Our target was reached, and it was another good trade. The entry price would have been 1116.00; however, I wanted a bar to close above resistance before entering the trade.

I would not recommend using only three indicators to trade with, nor would I recommend using so many that it becomes impossible to see all of them. But it would be wise to use the necessary ones to confirm the direction of the trend—and the entry.

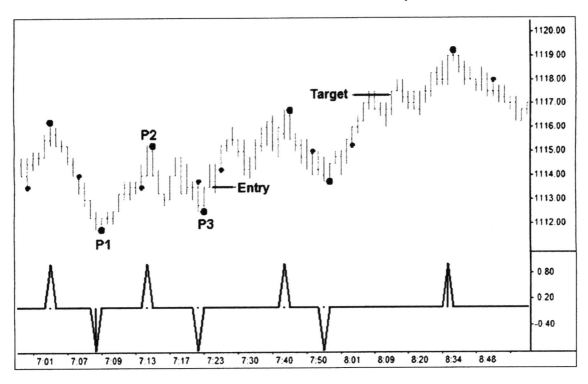

ES, 3000 Share Bar, July 8, 2004

P1=1111.75, P2=1115.25, and P3=1112.50. We had a major bottom at P1, then P2 formed, and then P3. We confirmed the trade using the Trigger Points indicator. The entry was at 1113.50, the stop was placed at 1112.00, and the target was placed at 1117.25. The market rallied up, reaching our target—another good trade.

Patience is needed to wait for these setups. Try not to force a trade. If you do, you most likely will regret it. You don't have to trade every day—even if you are "day trading". If there is not a setup for a few days, that's all right, you will have plenty of days with many good setups. Remember, I am keeping the charts very clean so you can clearly see the setups. Under normal trading conditions, I would be using a few more indicators than what you are seeing on these charts.

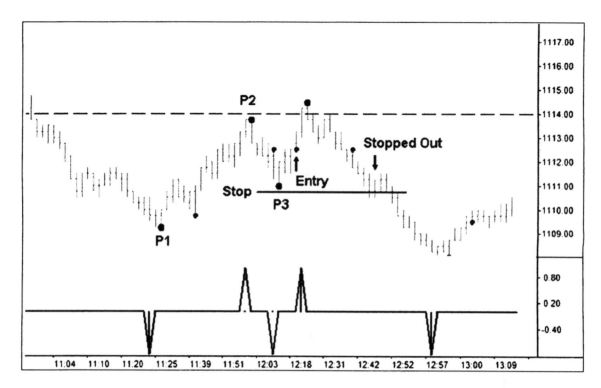

ES, 3000 Share Bar, July 8, 2004

P1=1109.25, P2=1113.75, and P3=1111.00. This is a "should I" or "should I not" kind of trade for most traders. Support one is at 1114.00, which became resistance after the price broke below and retested it. We had resistance at P2, and then P3 formed and the entry was confirmed. Had we taken this trade, the price would have moved up testing floor resistance and sold off rather quickly, stopping out at 1110.50, resulting in a loss of 1.75 points.

This is where your trading plan comes in. Would you, or would you not, take this trade after the market tested floor resistance at P2? It saves a lot of time and stress to have a plan in writing ahead of time. In other words, to avoid a spur-of-the-moment "should I" or "should I not" dilemma, it is always best to *have a trading plan, and trade the plan.*

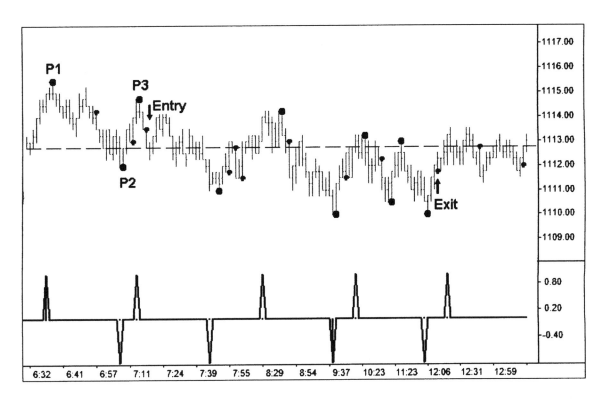

ES, 3000 Share Bar, July 9, 2004

P1=1115.50, P2=1112.00, and P3=1114.75. We had our usual short setup, and the entry price was 1113.25 due to slippage. The stop was at 1115.25. This was an unusual and boring trading day. All the market did was snake around the floor pivot all day. The price never made it to our target or our stop. Late in the afternoon, there was a new setup to enter long; however, it was too close to the end of the trading day for me to want to enter a long position. I would have exited the short trade a tick below my entry, grossing one tick (0.25)—enough to cover commissions, fees and still walk away with a small profit.

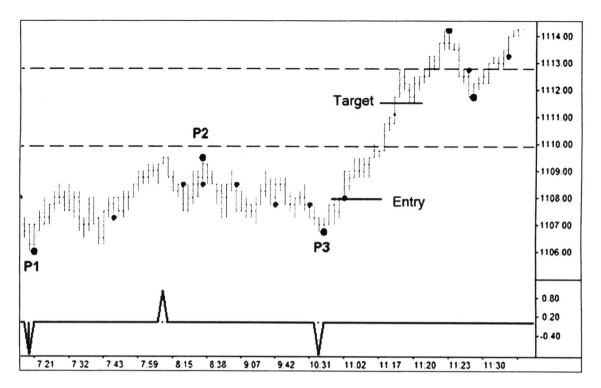

ES, 3000 Share Bar, July 12, 2004

P1=1106.00, P2=1109.50, and P3=1106.75. Here we see our normal setup for a long entry. The entry for the trade was at 1107.75, the stop was placed at 1106.25, and the profit target was placed at 1111.50. The market rallied up and the profit target was achieved. This trade would have grossed 3.75 points.

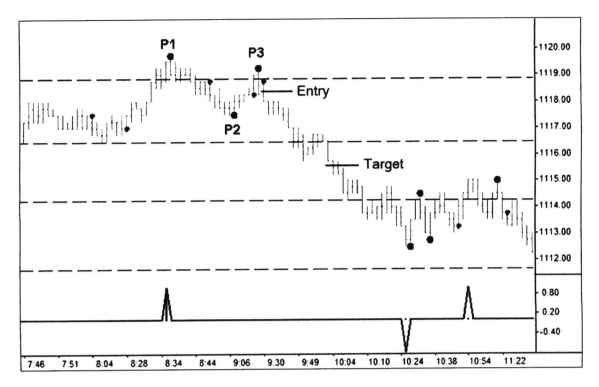

ES, 3000 Share Bar, July 14, 2004

P1=1119.75, P2=1117.50, and P3=1119.25. The dashed line at the top of the chart shows floor resistance. The entry price was 1118.50, the stop was placed at 1119.75, and the profit target was placed at 1115.50 using a 2.5:1 reward/risk ratio. The market sold off for a nice gross profit of 3.00 points minus commissions and exchange fees.

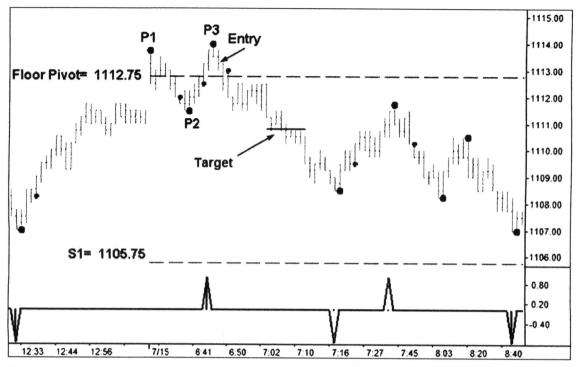

ES, 3000 Share Bar, July 14, 2004

P1=1113.75, P2=1111.50, and P3=1114.50. This is another "should I" or "should I not" type of trade. If it is part of your trading plan, then you would certainly want to take it. The only problem I see with this trade is the uncertainty of where to place a profit target. I couldn't get a good target based on P1 and P2. There was not enough price movement to justify such a small profit target compared to the stop of 1.25 points. Therefore, for someone to successfully trade this setup, a larger profit target would be needed. By placing the target in the 1110.75 area, a gross profit of 3.0 points could be attained if the market continued to sell off. In this case, the market did sell off reaching the target.

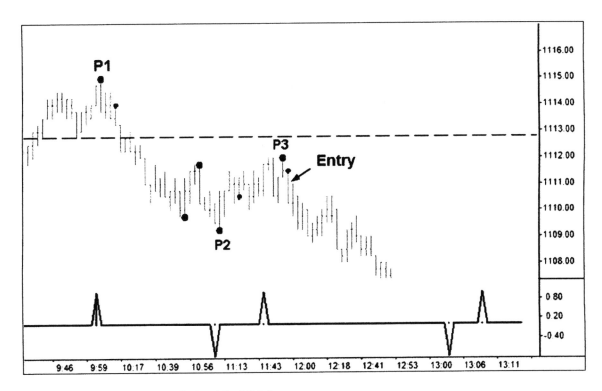

ES, 3000 Share Bar, July 15, 2004

P1=1115.00, P2=1109.25, and P3=1112.00. This was a nice setup; not only did we have good price movement between P1 and P2, we also had P3 test floor resistance at 1112.75. The trade would have been entered at 1110.50, the stop was placed at 1112.50, and the profit target was placed at 1105.50 using a ratio of 2.5:1. The market sold off for a nice profit of 5.0 points. The following chart will show the profit target and where the trade was exited.

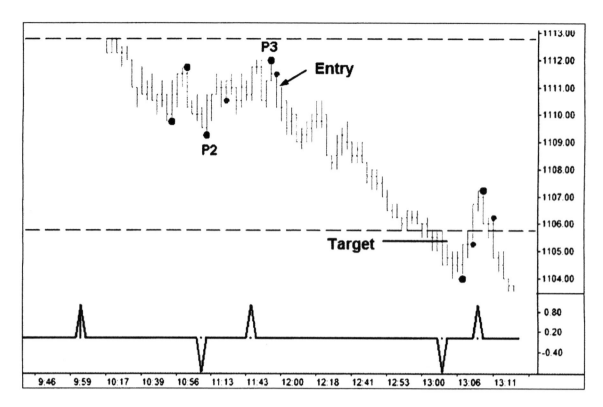

ES, 3000 Share Bar, July 15, 2004

This is the chart showing the exit of the trade from the previous page.

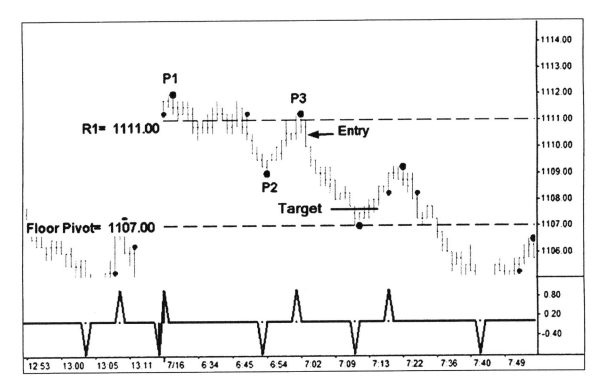

ES, 3000 Share Bar, July 16, 2004

P1=1112.00, P2=1109.00, and P3=1111.25.

Here is another favorable short setup right off of resistance one. The entry price was 1110.50, the stop was placed at 1111.75, and the profit target was placed at 1107.50. The market sold off nicely reaching the target for a gross profit of 3 points.

In the process of editing the book for reprint, I decided to add some new charts. I am now trading the ER2 (Russell 2000 E-mini), usually on a 233 or 377 tick chart. The main thing to look for when seeking a tradable market is that it has enough price movement between turn points to be profitable. Other than the market traded, the only other difference between the previous and the following charts is where I am placing the stop. I am placing the stop one tick from P3. The ER2 trades in 0.10 increments; therefore, one point equals one hundred USD.

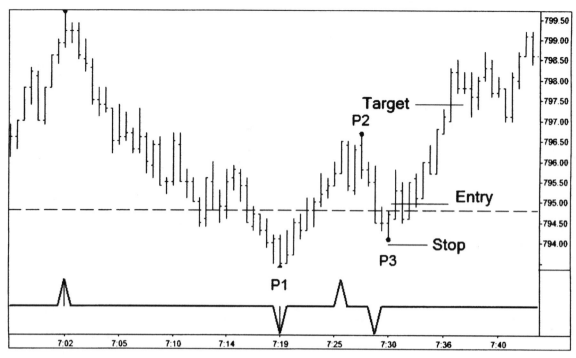

ER2, 233 Tick Bar, November 5, 2007

P1=793.40, P2=796.70, and P3=794.10. Here is another nice long setup. Right above support one the entry was triggered. The entry price was 794.90, the stop was placed at 794.00, and the profit target was placed at 797.30. The market rallied up reaching the target at 797.30 for a nice gross profit of 2.40 points per contact.

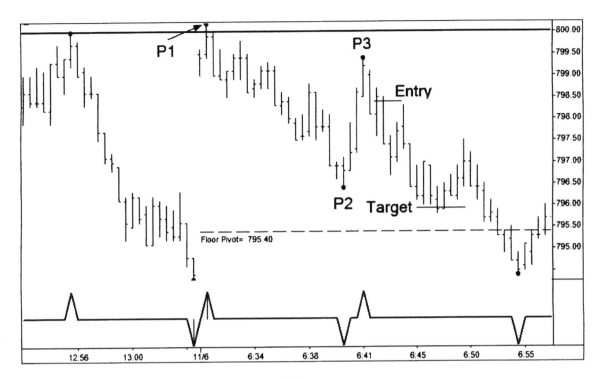

ER2, 233 Tick Bar, November 5, 2007

P1=800.20, P2=796.40, and P3=799.40. Here is another good short setup. The horizontal line toward the top of the chart was a line I drew to see what the high of P1 was in relation to the last turn point high of the previous day. I wanted to make sure that the close of P1 was below that previous high, and it was. Usually when the market gaps up, it is an indication of a strong market toward the upside. However, because the market sold off from the high, I was looking for a short setup. The entry price was 798.40, the stop was 799.50, and the target was placed at 795.70. The market sold off reaching the target with a nice 2.70 point gross profit.

ER2, 377 Tick Bar, January 2, 2008

P1=773.90, P2=766.20, and P3=771.60. This is the first day of trading for 2008, and not too long after the opening a promising short formed using P1 from the previous trading day of December 31, 2007. P2 formed just below the Floor Pivot at 767.70 and then the price moved up some; however, the price could not close above resistance one at 773.20. If the closing price did close above the high of P1, then the trade would have been negated. P3 setup nicely and the trade could have been entered at 769.70. The stop was placed at 771.70, and the target was 764.00. The market sold off in a hurry, reaching the target for a nice gross profit of 5.70.

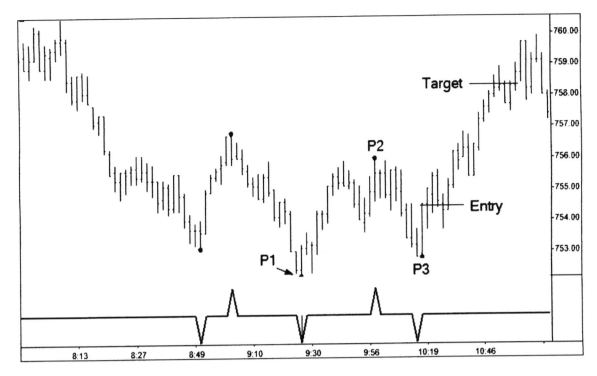

ER2, 377 Tick Bar, January 2, 2008

P1=752.20, P2=756.00, and P3=752.80. Here we have a long setup. The trigger for the entry was 753.80; however, due to slippage the fill would have been at 754.30. The stop was placed at 752.70 and the target was 758.30 (keeping with a 2.5:1 ratio). The market rallied up reaching the target for a 4 point gross profit.

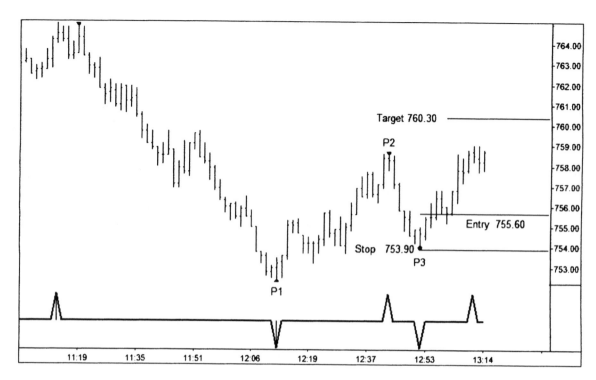

ER2, 377 Tick Bar, January 2, 2008

It's very common for most traders to wonder if the market will open to the upside, or downside. The majority of the time we can determine the direction of the opening by looking at the price patterns from the previous day.

P1=752.30, P2=758.70, and P3=754.00. Here we have a long setup going into the closing bell. Personally, I do not hold positions overnight, but this method of trading could be incorporated into a trader's trading plan. The entry price would be 755.60, the stop would have been placed at 753.90 and the calculated target was 760.30. The chart on the next page shows the results of this trade.

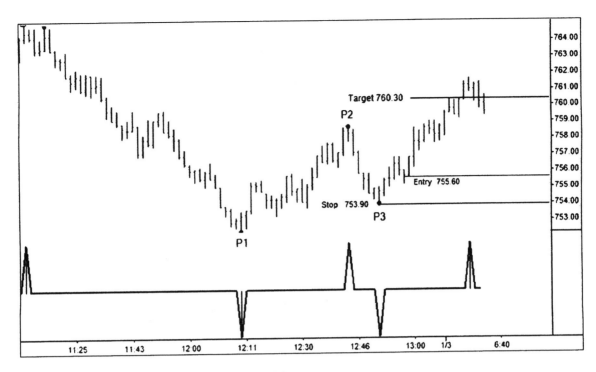

ER2, 377 Tick Bar, January 3, 2008

The market rallied up, reaching the target with a gross profit of 4.7 points.

On the previous two charts you can see that the stop, entry, and target were plotted on the chart. This is done using my Trident indicator, which is part of my software package. This indicator will work in real-time. Most of the charts shown in this book were plotted using the calculations built into this indicator.

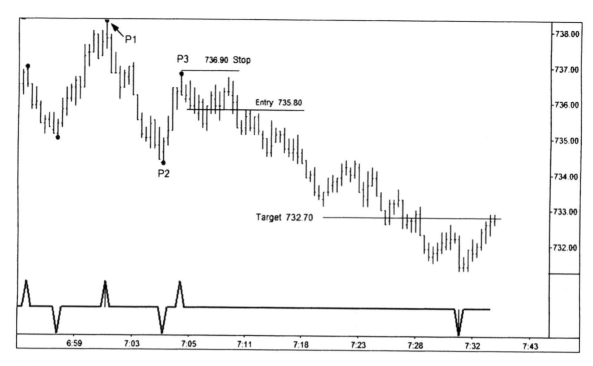

ER2, 144 Tick Bar, January 4, 2008

P1=738.30, P2=734.30, and P3=736.80. This is a 144 tick chart, which is a faster chart to trade than the 377 tick, or the ES charts used earlier in the book.

This was another classic setup. The entry was 735.80, the stop was 736.90, and the target was placed at 732.70. The market sold off, the target was attained, and resulted in a gross profit of 3.1 points.

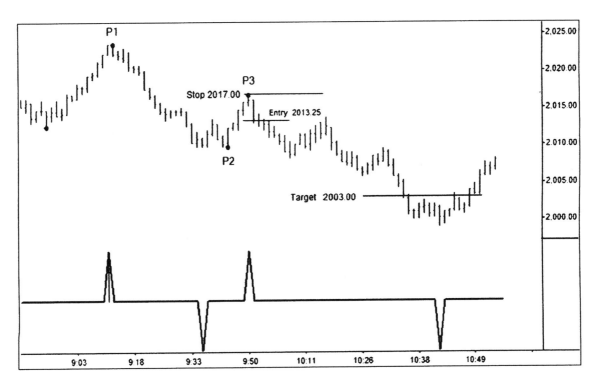

NQ, 233 Tick Bar, January 4, 2008

P1=2023.50, P2=2009.75, and P3=2016.75. This is a NASDAQ 100 E-Mini chart. This was another type of setup that I watch for. The entry was 2013.25, the stop was 2017.00, and the target was placed at 2003.00. The market sold off, the target was realized and the trade resulted in a gross profit of 10.25 points.

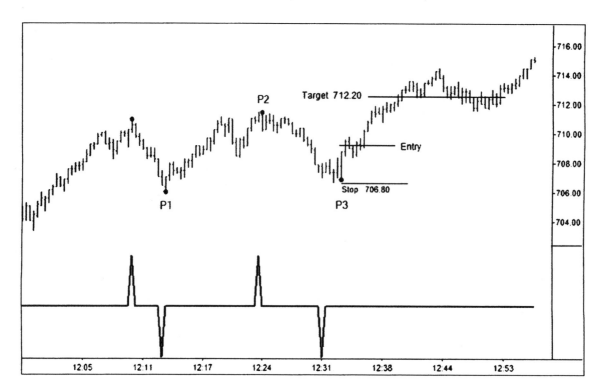

ER2, 233 Tick Bar, January 9, 2008

P1=706.10, P2=711.50, and P3=706.90. The trend is up; therefore, we would be looking for a long entry. The entry for this trade was 708.30, the stop was 706.80, and the target was placed at 712.20. The market rallied up and resulted in a gross profit of 3.90.

CHAPTER 16

Commencement Day

Developing Your Trading Skills

*T*his chapter is where you can test what you have learned, and thus help develop your trading skills. By working these exercises, coupled with what you have learned from this book, you will be well on your way to becoming a more confident and successful trader.

I will post the charts with the price of P1, P2, and P3. You will take it from there, deciding whether or not you will take the trade, and where your entry, stop, and target price should be. When calculating an entry for a short, I will round the entry price down to the nearest price. When calculating an entry for a long, I will round the entry price up to the nearest price. I will base the stop two ticks from P3, and the profit target will be determined based on what you have learned in the previous chapters. I will back the target off by one tick.

Remember that if the distance between P1 and P2 will give you too small of a target in relation to your stop, you will then use a target based on a 2.5:1 reward/risk ratio. *In this case you will not back the target off by a tick.* With this in mind, if the stop is very large, then it will be prudent to pass on that trade. The answers will be at the end of this chapter.

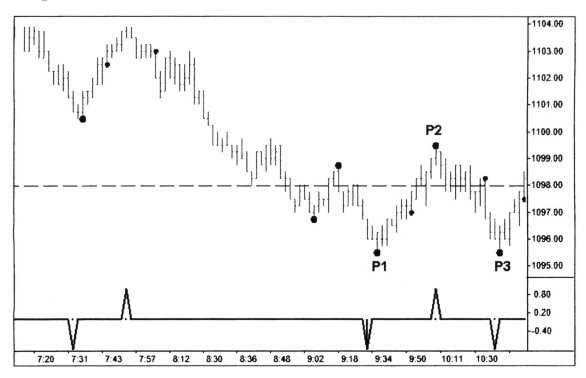

Chart 1; ES, 3000 Share Bar, July 19, 2004

P1=1095.50

P2=1099.50

P3=1095.50

Dashed line is support one at 1098.00.

Should you take this trade?

Entry=?

Stop=?

Profit Target=?

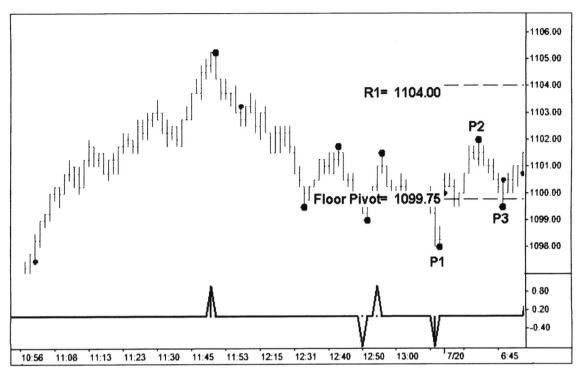

Chart (2) ES, 3000 Share Bar, July 20, 2004

P1=1098.00

P2=1102.00

P3=1099.50

Should you take this trade?

Entry=?

Stop=?

Profit Target=?

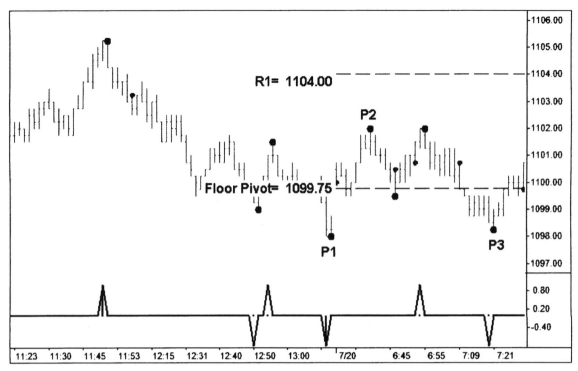

Chart (3) ES, 3000 Share Bar, July 20, 2004

P1=1098.00

P2=1102.00

P3=1098.25

Should you take this trade?

Entry=?

Stop=?

Profit Target=?

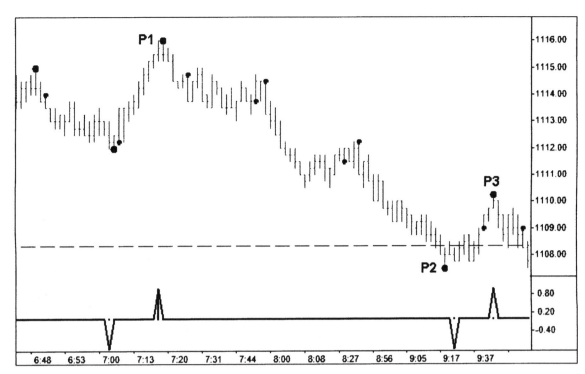

Chart (4) ES, 3000 Share Bar, July 21, 2004

P1=1116.00

P2=1107.50

P3=1110.25

Should you take this trade?

Entry=?

Stop=?

Profit Target=?

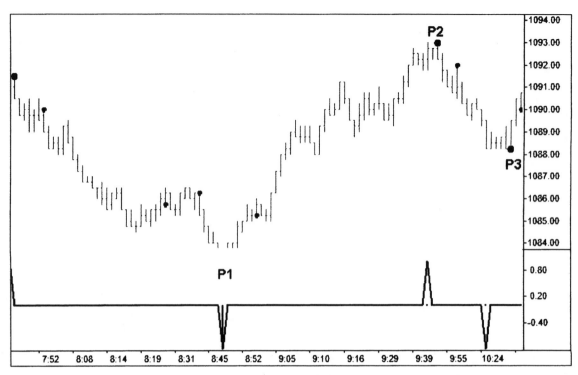

Chart (5) ES, 3000 Share Bar, July 22, 2004

P1=1083.00

P2=1093.00

P3=1088.25

Should you take this trade?

Entry=?

Stop=?

Profit Target=?

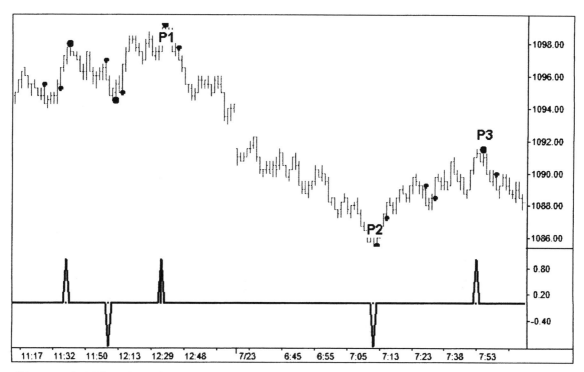

Chart (6) ES, 3000 Share Bar, July 23, 2004

P1=1099.25

P2=1085.50

P3=1091.50

Should you take this trade?

Entry=?

Stop=?

Profit Target=?

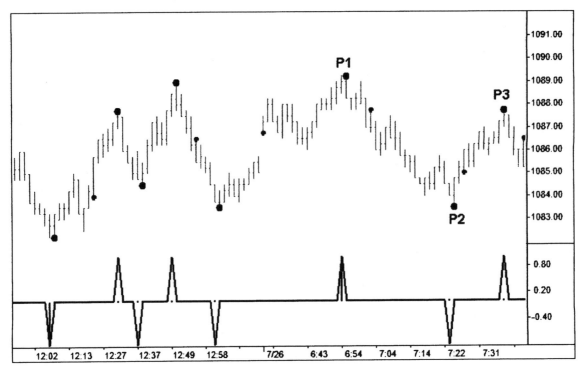

Chart (7) ES, 3000 Share Bar, July 26, 2004

P1=1089.25

P2=1083.50

P3=1087.75

Should you take this trade?

Entry=?

Stop=?

Profit Target=?

Answers for chart review

The trades shown on charts 5 and 6 would not have reached the target, so you would have exited these trades before the close of the market unless you wanted to hold the position overnight. In these two examples, the trades were exited right at market close.

Chart 1

Yes
Entry = 1096.50
Stop = 1095.00
Profit Target = 1100.25
Winning trade, + 3.75 points

Chart 2

Yes
Entry = 1100.50
Stop = 1099.00
Profit Target = 1104.25
Losing trade, - 1.50 points

Chart 3

Yes
Entry = 1099.25
Stop = 1097.75
Profit Target = 1103.00
Winning trade, + 3.75 points

Chart 4

Yes
Entry = 1108.00
Stop = 1110.75
Profit Target = 1099.75
Winning trade, + 8.25 points

Chart 5

Yes
Entry = 1090.75
Stop = 1087.75
Profit Target = 1098.00
Winning trade, MOC + 3.25 points
(MOC is market order on close)

Chart 6

Yes
Entry =1088.00
Stop = 1092.00
Profit Target = 1078.00
Winning trade, MOC + 3.00 points

Chart 7

Yes
Entry = 1086.25
Stop = 1088.25
Profit Target = 1080.75
Winning trade, + 5.50 points

Summary

Win/Loss Ratio was 6:1. Total number of points made was 26. Largest winning trade was 8.25 points. Largest losing trade was 1.50 points.

I didn't allow for commissions, or slippage. However, slippage is usually not a problem if you use limit orders. Occasionally you will have some slippage on your stop.

APPENDIX A

Products and services:

Trend Pro Inc.

2533 N. Carson Street Suite T326
Carson City, NV 89706
E-mail: support@trendpro.com
Web Site: www.trendpro.com

Products and services offered:

Custom Trading Software
Seminars
Educational Trading courses

Brokers and Charting Programs

For a current list of recommended brokers and charting programs, check my
website at: www.trendpro.com.

APPENDIX B

Roy Kelly's Indicators	Approximate Alternative
Kelly's Cycle Identifier	None
Two Smooth	Fast Stochastic
Floor Pivots	Floor Pivots
Swing H/L	Swing H/L
Trend Lines	Trend Lines
Filtered Waves	None
Kelly's Advance MA	None
Turn Points	None
Trident	None

There is no substitute for the real thing; however, I do not want anyone to feel obligated to buy my custom indicators. If you would like more information on my custom indicators, or you decide you would like to incorporate them into your trading plan and would like to place an order, you can visit our website at (www.trendpro.com).

I have found it most helpful to use custom indicators. However, you personally must decide which tools you will use in conjunction with your trading plan.

APPENDIX C

TRACK RECORD OF WINNING PERCENTAGE					
Date	Winners	Losers	Total	Wins%	Accum. %

Index